GoodFood magazine

Christmas
Made Easy

Mary Cadogan is a highly respected cookery writer with a wealth of experience in many areas of the food world. Before joining *BBC Good Food Magazine*, Mary contributed to several national magazines and was a top food stylist specialising in food photography. She is also the author of several best-selling cookery books. Mary was appointed Deputy Editor of *Good Food* in 1993 and since then, in addition to writing her popular food features in the magazine, she has been responsible for ensuring that all the recipes taste great, work perfectly and are beautifully photographed. She is now Food Director of both *Good Food Magazine* and the new BBC food magazine, *Olive*.

Mary's Acknowledgements:
I'm grateful to all the chefs who have allowed us to reproduce their recipes in this book. In particular I would like to thank Darina Allen, Rosa Baden-Powell, Val Barrett, Mary Berry, Raymond Blanc, Lorna Brash, Ross Burden, Antonio Carluccio, Maxine Clark, Shona Crawford Poole, Gilly Cubitt, Joanna Farrow, Silvana Franco, Moyra Fraser, Paul Gayler, Brian Glover, Ainsley Harriott, Henry Harris, Alastair Hendy, James Martin, Nick Nairn, Merrilees Parker, Ann Payne, Gordon Ramsay, Paul and Jeanne Rankin, Simon Rimmer, Rick Stein, Tony Tobin, John Torode, Phil Vickery, Gregg Wallace and Ruth Watson.

I'd also like to thank Melanie Leyshon, who compiled the book for me, and the whole team at *Good Food Magazine* for all their recipe ideas, help and testing, including Sara Buenfeld, Barney Desmazery, Orlando Murrin, Angela Nilsen and Jeni Wright.

Published by BBC Books, BBC Worldwide Ltd,
Woodlands, 80 Wood Lane, London W12 0TT

This edition produced for
The Book People Ltd, Hall Wood Avenue,
Haydock, St Helens WA11 9UL

First published in 2004

ISBN: 0 563 52237 2

Compiled by Melanie Leyshon

Commissioning Editor: Vivien Bowler
Project Editor for BBC Books: Rachel Copus
Designer: Kathryn Gammon
Production Controller: Christopher Tinker

Set in Helvetica Neue
Printed and bound in Singapore by Tien Wah Press
Colour separations by Radstock Reproductions, Midsomer Norton

GoodFood
magazine

Christmas
Made Easy

Edited by Mary Cadogan

TED SMART

Contents

Introduction

Christmas is my favourite time in the cookery calendar. Coming from a large family, I love the many entertaining opportunities it offers, from having friends around for a pre-Christmas supper and drinks, to the large traditional family Christmas lunch. I'm usually cooking for at least a dozen on Christmas Day every year.

Christmas is always such a big cooking occasion, whether it's your first Christmas as host or your 25th. As Food Director of *BBC Good Food* magazine I've cooked more Christmasses than most. I play a key part in planning and creating Christmas recipes for the magazine every August, demonstrate them at the *BBC Good Food Show* in November, then I cook the Christmas meal for real for my family every December. So you could say I'm truly experienced.

Over the years I've had the wonderful opportunity to devise my own festive dishes to share with *Good Food* readers and to work with all your favourite celebrity chefs. And here are my top Christmas choices, gathered together in this one Christmas book. They're from some of the country's best loved food names, the *BBC Good Food* cookery team and top contributors.

Between us, the cooks and chefs in this book have years of experience of cooking Christmas, so rest assured you're in inspired and safe hands, and will be cooking with help from the best in the business. We will help make this Christmas taste the best ever.

While all the recipes are extra special, we've made sure that they are straightforward, too. You'll find step-by-step photographs and clever tips to help you achieve fantastic results.

All the recipes are simple and enjoyable to cook, but they'll still impress your guests. Each one would look at home in a top restaurant, but you don't require the skills of a top chef, or any expensive catering equipment, to recreate them at home. They've also been put through their paces many times, having been thoroughly tried and tested in the *BBC Good Food* test kitchen. These recipes really do work ...

So your kitchen doesn't become your second home this Christmas, I've included a cunning batch of freeze-ahead and prepare-ahead recipes. No one will guess they've been sitting in your freezer all the while. The secret of a successful Christmas is in the planning, so we've included a two-month calendar (page 8). It will help you organise your pre-Christmas food shopping and preparations, and avoid those last-minute panics like no ice for the G&Ts. Plus, we have included a mail order list of our favourite suppliers.

Cooking is much more fun when you don't have to go out and shop for every ingredient. Shop for the fun stuff – visiting your local cheese shop, deli and bakery, not forgetting those farmers' markets that are springing up all over the country – leave the heavy stuff for the supermarket to deliver.

In this book, you'll find recipes for every Christmas occasion, from light nibbles for a drinks party to the Christmas Day menu, which will suit the beginner and the more experienced cook alike. But before you get carried away and want to cook everything, make a list. Mix and match what you'd like to make and buy, including some ready-made items from our suggested suppliers, your deli or supermarket.

And while we're feeling sensible, don't turn down any offers of help either. Part of the fun of Christmas is joining in and helping out, and don't forget to delegate – the sprouts won't spoil if someone else peels them.

Christmas is for all to enjoy and share, including you. We've provided the inspiration for the food, now go out and celebrate the festive season.

Here's raising a glass of bubbly to your best Christmas ever.

Mary Cadogan

Mary Cadogan

Christmas-made-easy Planner

A two-month, week-by-week guide to preparing for the Big Day

November

1st week in November

■ Sort out your freezer, and aim to use up surplus stocks to make room for festive goodies. Take stock of your storecupboards too, throwing away out-of-date herbs and spices.

■ Stock up on dried fruits and nuts if you're making the Festive Fruit and Nut Cake (page 14) and Christmas Pud with a Twist (page 20). Your cakes and puds will taste much better with fresh supplies.

■ Buy stock cubes, bouillon and check flours, salt and whole black peppercorns, honeys, preserves and conserves.

■ Stock up on cookery basics like greaseproof paper, cling film, foil, freezer bags and check your cookery utensils and equipment. Make sure you have enough plastic containers – with lids – for storing freeze-ahead meals and leftovers.

2nd week in November

■ Make your Christmas cake and pudding. Check out the recipes in our Get a Headstart for Christmas chapter (chapter 1) and start making your mincemeat, chutneys and mince pies for the freezer.

■ If you haven't already, finalise plans for Christmas lunch, and the all-important guestlist.

■ Once the guestlist is confirmed, check our turkey serving chart (page 68) and order your Christmas bird.

3rd week in November

■ Get online to check out the wine and Champagne deals, or take a trip to your local off-licence or France. Stock up now as there will be plenty of special offers around, especially on Champagne.

■ Stock up on mixers and soft drinks and keep your supplies tucked away out of sight.

■ Think about your festive table; buy crackers, napkins, candles and decorations.

4th week in November

■ As you've been using up foods in your freezer, check our Freeze Ahead section in chapter 1 and start making puddings or dishes for entertaining, not forgetting to label and date them.

■ Take a trip abroad to a Christmas market or look out for farmers' markets near you to buy home-made preserves, conserves and foodie gifts.

December

1st week in December

■ If you've been feeding your cake with brandy, it should now be nice and boozy and ready for icing. Set aside an afternoon to decorate it.

■ Post your Christmas cards second class this week and breathe a huge sigh of relief.

■ Still time to stock up the freezer. Check out our dessert collection and aim to make one stunning pud or main course.

■ Talk to your florist about ordering a centrepiece for the dining table or think about making your own and putting in an order for blooms. See our Festive Table setting (page 70).

■ Send out invites for friends to come around in the next two weeks as you're so organised!

2nd week in December

■ Aim to get all your presents and giftwrapping finished this week, as this puts you in a strong position to relax and socialise in the build up to Christmas.

■ Ask friends over and serve a Freeze-Ahead menu or make our Celebration Canapés (page 48).

■ Buy extras with your shopping this week, such as chocolates, nuts and basics for your freezer such as ice, cranberries, ice cream, garlic bread and ready-made frozen desserts and canapés.

■ Hang the Christmas wreath on the door to let everyone know Christmas has officially started at your home.

■ Everything is so under control invite the neighbours round for mulled wine and a batch of mince pies you have defrosted overnight and warmed through in the oven.

■ Make your brandy butter and store wrapped in the fridge.

■ Check your most glamorous apron is clean and pressed and you have plenty of clean tea towels, oven gloves and rubber gloves for any willing guests who volunteer to wash up.

3rd week in December

■ The real fun begins. Make a final shopping list of last-minute items such as fresh produce. You'll be surprised how little there is left to get. But don't forget basics like milk and breads, cream, salad, vegetables, fruit and any condiments, mayonnaise, mustards, pâtés, sauces or pickles you haven't made.

■ Sort out the fridge, banishing half-finished, never-going-to-be-used items to the bin. This is no time for hangers-on when space is tight.

4th week in December

■ Go and buy three or four of the most delectable wedges of cheese from the best cheese shop you can get to. Also buy extras like cheese biscuits, cantuccini biscuits, panettone, mulled wine kits and good quality dark roasted coffee at the deli.

■ Throw our Last-minute Drinks Party (page 58).

■ Your turkey should be ready for collection around the 23rd/24th or should be winging its way to you. Check all's well with your supplier.

■ Christmas Eve, check out our timeplan to the Big Day on page 66. Relax, if you've followed our week-by-week plan you're in for the most enjoyable Christmas ever!

CHAPTER 1

Get a Headstart for Christmas

Christmas is a magical time and remains the food event of the year. **Make it special and stress-free** by not having to conjure up those big-occasion meals from scratch. At Christmas we have more family and friends descend on us than at any other time of the year, so it helps to be prepared.

Whether this is your first Christmas or your fifteenth, start preparing a few recipes a month or two ahead so you have the key culinary Christmas classics all wrapped up, **leaving you more time to relax** and enjoy adding the finishing touches. Don't forget, Christmas should be fun for cooks too!

Two recipes that are a must at Christmas are the cake and pudding. Fortunately, not only can these be made months ahead, they will taste better for doing so as their flavours mingle and mature. If you plan a leisurely afternoon baking, cooking becomes a pleasure,

not a chore against the clock, and you can enjoy those festive aromas a month or two early. As well as the **traditional boozy fruit cake**, we've included a **cherry Christmas cake** for those who prefer something lighter.

A few weeks' ahead is the best time to make your **mincemeat** too. Set it aside in jars, ready to be transformed into mince pies or presented as gifts nearer the big day. But don't feel you have to make absolutely everything, if making pastry isn't your thing, buy a ready-rolled version and put the creative work into the design and decoration.

For those with a savoury tooth, we've included Mary Berry's delicious **Christmas chutney** (page 13). It's the perfect accompaniment to the Boxing Day cold meats. The great thing about these recipes is that it doesn't matter if you don't use them up as they will keep into the new year.

Ruth Watson's
Boozy Mincemeat

Home-made mincemeat is so much better than ready-made. It's also a doddle to make. This recipe is wonderfully boozy and nicely spicy. Don't stint on the alcohol as this preserves the mincemeat and stops it going mouldy. The secret is to wash and dry all the dried fruit thoroughly. Packed into attractive jars, it makes a great gift.

Time: 30–40 minutes, plus 24 hours standing

Makes 3.5kg/7lb

500g/1lb 2oz currants

500g/1lb 2oz muscatel raisins or Californian raisins (or a mixture)

500g/1lb 2oz sultanas

500g/1lb 2oz Bramley apples, peeled, cored and chopped fairly small

2 x 250g boxes shredded beef suet

100g/4oz whole blanched almonds, coarsely chopped

350g/12oz natural demerara sugar

100g/4oz muscovado sugar

1 rounded tsp ground cinnamon

2 rounded tsp ground mixed spice

1 large, juicy lemon

250g/9oz whole mixed peel, chopped into small dice

125ml/4fl oz dark rum

125ml/4fl oz Disaronno Originale liqueur (amaretto)

175ml/6fl oz French brandy

STEP 1 Wash the dried fruit thoroughly in a colander under the cold tap (you may find it easier to do this in batches). Tip the fruit on to clean tea towels and dry by patting in the cloths. Put the dried fruit in a very large bowl with the apples, suet, almonds, sugars and spices. Grate the zest of the lemon into the bowl, then squeeze in the juice. Tip in the peel and the alcohol.

STEP 2 Mix all the ingredients very thoroughly – it's easiest to do this with your (very clean) hands. Cover and leave to stand for 24 hours, asking the family to stop and give it a good stir with a spoon when they pass by. Pack the mincemeat into sterilised or dishwasher-clean jars and top with greaseproof paper jam covers. Seal the jars tightly and store in a cool, dark place. Although mincemeat will last from one year to the next, use it within 6 months.

STERILISING JARS
Use ovenproof jars only such as jam jars with plastic not metal-coated lids or Kilner jars with plastic seals. Wash the jars and lids in hot soapy water, then rinse and dry. Place in a heated oven at 150°C/Gas 2/fan oven 130°C for 10 minutes to sterilise. Carefully remove for filling.

CANDIED PEEL
The flavour and quality of whole strips of candied peel is so much better than ready-chopped. It's well worth the extra effort of chopping the peel yourself, although you might find it easier snipping it into small chunks with kitchen scissors.

Mary Berry's
Christmas Chutney

Chutneys are supposed to mature, but this one never has a chance because it gets eaten too quickly. This happens every year and I often end up having to make another batch – so be warned! It's the perfect match for cheese and cold meats and is truly delicious in turkey sandwiches. It's also brilliant if you're making a sauce to go with chicken, turkey or steak – simply add a spoonful or two to pep up the flavour and to make it instantly Christmassy.

Time: 2–2¼ hours

Makes about 2.5kg/6lb

900g/2lb tomatoes

1 large aubergine, 1 green pepper and 3 red peppers (total weight about 900g/2lb)

700g/1lb 9oz onions, peeled and fairly finely chopped, by hand or in a food processor

4 fat garlic cloves, crushed

350g/12oz granulated sugar

300ml/½ pint white wine vinegar or distilled malt vinegar

1 tbsp salt

1 tbsp coriander seeds, crushed

1 tbsp paprika

2 tsp cayenne pepper

STEP 1 Peel the tomatoes – prick them with a sharp knife, pop in a bowl and cover with boiling water. Leave for a few seconds, drain and cover with cold water then peel. Chop the tomatoes and aubergine and seed and chop the peppers.

STEP 2 Put the chopped tomatoes and vegetables into a heavy-based pan with the onions and garlic; bring to the boil. Cover, lower the heat and simmer for 1 hour, stirring until tender. Add the sugar, vinegar, salt, coriander, paprika and cayenne and bring to the boil, stirring, until the sugar has dissolved. Boil for 30 minutes, or until the mixture achieves a chunky consistency and the watery liquid has evaporated.

STEP 3 Towards the end of the cooking time continue stirring so that the chutney doesn't catch on the bottom of the pan. Ladle the chutney into sterilised or dishwasher-clean jars (Kilner jars are ideal) and top with greaseproof paper jam covers. Seal the jars while still hot. Leave to mature for at least a month in a cool dark place.

Sara Buenfeld's
Festive Fruit and Nut Cake

Apart from being totally scrumptious, this cake is baked with a new syrup and nut topping – a bit like a Florentine biscuit – so all you have to do is tie round a ribbon. If you still favour the traditional approach, however, it's easy to make the cake without the topping and simply marzipan and ice it in the usual way. See our cake decorating ideas on pages 130–139.

Time: 30–40 minutes, plus 2 hours in the oven

Cuts into 12–16 slices

*Freeze for up to 2 months

FOR THE CAKE

250g/9oz butter, at room temperature

140g/5oz light muscovado sugar

6 large eggs, beaten

280g/10oz plain flour

85g/3oz ground almonds

2 tsp ground ginger

2 tsp ground cinnamon

700g/1lb 9oz luxury mixed fruit (including raisins, currants, sultanas, mixed peel and glacé cherries)

3 tbsp dark rum

140g/5oz white marzipan, diced

FOR THE FLORENTINE TOPPING (optional)

50g/2oz each whole skinned hazelnuts and blanched almonds

85g/3oz each brazil nuts and flaked almonds

140g/5oz whole glacé cherries

100g/4oz golden syrup

TO DECORATE

1 metre of wide ribbon

FOR THE ICING (optional)

140g/5oz icing sugar

egg white or cold water

STEP 1 Preheat the oven to 180°C/gas 4/fan oven 160°C and lightly grease and line the base and sides of a deep 20cm/8in round loose-based cake tin with Bake-o-Glide or baking parchment. Beat the butter, sugar, eggs, flour, ground almonds and spices until thoroughly mixed and creamy, preferably with an electric beater or in a food mixer. If you are making the florentine topping, measure off 100g/4oz of the cake mixture, put in a bowl and set aside.

STEP 2 Fold the fruit and rum into the remaining mixture, then gently stir in the marzipan. Spoon this mixture into the prepared cake tin and flatten with a spatula to make a smooth even surface, then make a slight dip in the centre of the cake. This simple trick will give the finished cake a nice flat top. Bake for 1¼ hours. *(If you are not going to make our Florentine topping and prefer to ice your cake in the traditional way, cover the partly cooked cake with foil at this stage and bake for another 15–20 minutes or until cooked through, testing with a skewer as described in step 4, overleaf.)*

continued ▷

STEP 3 If you are going to make the fruit and nut topping you can do this while the cake is in the oven. Mix all the nuts, cherries and syrup into the remaining cake mixture. Spoon the mixture on top of the part-cooked cake (once it has had its 1¼ hours), evenly distributing the mixture of nuts and cherries across the surface of the cake. Loosely cover the top of the tin with foil.

STEP 4 Return to the oven for 40 minutes more, then take off the foil and bake for another 10–15 minutes, so the nuts can turn golden. Keep an eye on them, so they don't get too dark. To test the cake mixture is cooked, insert a fine skewer into the cake – if it comes out clean then it's ready. Cool in the tin then turn out, keeping the lining on, and wrap with foil. (*The cake will keep for up to 2 weeks or can be frozen for up to 2 months.*) To serve, remove the cake from the foil and strip away the lining. Place on a board or serving plate and tie with a decorative ribbon.

To add the final touch to the Florentine topping, try this easy finish. Sift the icing sugar into a bowl, then stir in the egg white or cold water, a little at a time, until you have a smooth icing that drizzles easily from the tip of a dessert spoon. Drizzle over the fruit and nut topping, then leave to set for an hour. The cake will keep for 2 days, loosely covered with cling film, although the icing won't look as fresh and white.

LINING THE CAKE TIN

It's important to line your tin correctly as it protects the cake and stops it from sticking. Cut a double thickness strip of baking parchment or greaseproof paper 5cm (2in) deeper than your tin and long enough to wrap around it with a slight overlap. Make a 2.5cm (1in) crease along the folded edge, then snip up to the crease at intervals to make a fringe.

Cut two rounds of paper to fit the base of the tin. Grease the tin, put one of the rounds of paper in the base, then grease the paper. Now fit the long strip of paper round the sides of the tin with the fringed edge flat on the base.

Fit the second round over the top.

Sara Buenfeld's
Orange-scented Marzipan

The generous amount of ground almonds and the orange zest in this recipe give it the edge over sweet shop-bought varieties. This quantity of marzipan will cover the sides and top of Sara Buenfeld's Festive Fruit and Nut Cake on page 14, or see our tip, below, for turning it into delicious petits fours.

Time: 10–15 minutes

Covers a 22–23cm/9in round cake

This recipe contains raw egg

*Freeze for up to 6 weeks

280g/10oz ground almonds

140g/5oz golden caster sugar

140g/5oz icing sugar

grated zest of 1 orange

1 large egg, beaten

STEP 1 Tip the almonds and caster sugar into a large bowl. Sift the icing sugar on top and stir in along with the grated orange zest.

STEP 2 Add the egg and stir it into the almonds and sugar with the blade of a knife until roughly mixed, then knead lightly with your hands to bring the mixture together to a soft and pliable marzipan.

STEP 3 Wrap in cling film and keep in a cool place until needed. It will keep for up to a week like this in the fridge, or 6 weeks in the freezer.

AFTER-DINNER PETITS FOURS
It takes no time to transform the marzipan into petits fours. Halve the recipe, roll out the marzipan on a worksurface and cut into shapes such as diamonds, crescents and squares. Dip the shapes into quality melted chocolate, such as Green and Black's plain chocolate, and leave to set.

Orlando Murrin's
Light Cherry Christmas Cake

My mother has been making this lovely, light American cake since I was born, and it's still a favourite. It tastes so much better than any cake you can buy. I've updated it by creating a simple but stunning no-ice decoration. Tie an attractive ribbon around it for that festive finishing touch.

Time: 30 minutes, plus 2 hours in the oven and 30 minutes cooling

Cuts into 14 slices

250g/9oz butter, softened

200g/8oz light muscovado sugar

4 eggs

200g/8oz plain flour, sifted

300g/10oz currants

85g/3oz pecans, chopped

170g packet dried berries and cherries

200g/8oz glacé cherries, quartered

100g/4oz whole, mixed citrus peel, chopped

½ tsp freshly grated nutmeg

1½ tsp ground cinnamon

3 tbsp whisky or brandy

TO DECORATE

3 tbsp apricot jam

8 glacé cherries

caster sugar, for frosting

whole citrus peel (such as Sundora), cut into thin slices

pecan nut halves

thin red ribbon

1 Preheat the oven to 150°C/Gas 2/fan oven 130°C. Grease and line a 20cm/8in loose-bottomed cake tin that is at least 9cm/3½in deep with greased greaseproof paper or baking parchment. Cream the butter with the sugar until soft.

2 Beat in the eggs one at a time, then fold in the flour. Tip in the currants, pecans, dried berries and cherries, glacé cherries, citrus peel, nutmeg and cinnamon. Stir in the whisky or brandy, mix well.

3 Spoon the mixture into the tin. Flatten the mixture with the back of a spoon before tapping the tin sharply on a worktop to settle the contents. Make a smooth depression in the centre to help the cake rise evenly. Bake for 1 hour, cover loosely with foil and bake for a further hour until a skewer inserted into the centre comes out clean. Leave for 30 minutes to cool, then turn out, with the paper on. When cold, remove paper, rewrap in cling film and keep in an airtight container.

TO DECORATE

1 Dissolve the jam in 2 tablespoons of water, press through a sieve and brush the top of the cake generously with the glaze.

2 Roll the glacé cherries in a little caster sugar and arrange with citrus peel slices and a few pecan halves on the cake, so they stick to the glaze. Glaze the nuts, then tie the ribbon around the cake.

STORING THE CAKE

You can eat this cake almost at once, but it will keep for up to 2 months without the decoration. Wrap it in greaseproof paper and store in an airtight tin. Decorate the day before you plan to serve it.

Sara Buenfeld's
Christmas Pud with a Twist

Some cooks like to make their Christmas pud in November, and if this includes you, try this new passion fruit and Cointreau version which can be made and frozen a month ahead of Christmas, or steamed up to a week before you want to eat it. The steaming time for this recipe is half that of a traditional pudding too, so you only need to stay in for a few hours, wrapping presents perhaps, while it happily bubbles away. To make it even more irresistible, serve it with a tipsy pecan and Cointreau sauce.

Time: 1–1¼ hours, plus 3 hours steaming

Serves 10

*Freeze for up to 1 month

250g packet mixed dried fruits with apricot and passion fruit (we used Sainsbury's Way to Five)

175g/6oz ready-to-eat stoned dates, roughly chopped

85g/3oz dried cranberries

1 tbsp freshly grated root ginger

grated zest and juice of 1 large orange

100ml/3½fl oz Cointreau or Grand Marnier

100g/4oz butter, at room temperature

100g/4oz dark muscovado sugar

2 large eggs, beaten

50g/2oz self-raising flour

85g/3oz fresh white breadcrumbs

1 tsp ground cinnamon

85g/3oz pecan nuts, roughly chopped

PECAN TOPPING AND SAUCE

100g/4oz butter

100g/4oz light muscovado sugar

50g/2oz pecan nuts

50g/2oz dried cranberries

juice of 1 orange

3 tbsp Cointreau or Grand Marnier

sprig of fresh holly

icing sugar, for dusting

thick double cream, to serve

STEP 1 Put the dried fruits, dates, cranberries and ginger in a pan with the orange zest and juice, and the orange liqueur, then warm gently for 10 minutes, stirring occasionally, until the juices are absorbed and the mixture looks sticky. Set aside to cool.

STEP 2 Lightly grease a 1.3 litre/2¼ pint pudding basin, and line the base with a small disc of greaseproof paper. Beat the butter, sugar, eggs and flour together in a food mixer or large bowl until creamy, then stir in the cooled fruits, breadcrumbs, cinnamon and nuts. Spoon the mixture into the pudding basin, cover the bowl with greaseproof paper and foil, and tie on securely with string.

STEP 3 Put a long strip of folded foil under the basin and bring it up round the sides so that you can use it as a handle to lift the pudding in and out. Put the basin in a large pan and pour a kettle of boiling water into the pan so it comes halfway up the bowl, then cover and steam for 3 hours, topping up with boiling water every now and then. Leave it to cool, then store in a cool place for up to 1 week or freeze for 1 month.

STEP 4 The sauce can be made up to a day ahead. Melt the butter and sugar together in a frying pan. Tip in the pecans and cook, stirring, for a minute or two to toast them. Add the cranberries, orange juice and liqueur and continue to bubble until rich and syrupy. Cool, then tip into a bowl, cover and chill until ready to eat.

TO SERVE

1 Steam the pudding in a pan of boiling water for 1 hour to warm it through.

2 Put the pecan sauce in a pan, and gently warm through until melted and bubbling. Meanwhile, turn out the pudding. Peel the lining paper from the pudding and pile the nuts and cranberries from the sauce on top, and then generously spoon over the buttery sauce. Decorate with holly and dust lightly with icing sugar. Serve the pudding with the sauce and cream.

ALTERNATIVE SAUCE

If you prefer to serve classic brandy butter instead of the pecan sauce, cream 100g/4oz butter with 85g/3oz golden caster sugar and 50g/2oz light muscovado sugar. Beat in 4 tablespoons brandy, spoon into a dish and fork attractively. (This can be made up to 2 weeks ahead or frozen.)

Orlando Murrin's
Unbelievably Easy Mince Pies

If you find pastry tricky, this mince pie recipe is for you. However hard you treat it, the pastry will turn out crispy and biscuity. You don't even have to roll it out, just press the bases and tops out by hand.

Time: 30 minutes, plus 20 minutes in the oven

Makes 18 pies

*Freeze uncooked for up to 1 month

225g/8oz cold butter, diced

350g/12oz plain flour

100g/4oz golden caster sugar

280g/10oz mincemeat

1 small egg, beaten

icing sugar, for dusting

STEP 1 To make the pastry, rub the butter into the flour, then mix in the sugar and a pinch of salt. Combine the pastry into a ball – don't add any liquid – and knead it briefly. The dough will be fairly firm, like shortbread dough. You can use the dough immediately, or chill for later.

STEP 2 Preheat the oven to 200°C/Gas 6/fan oven 180°C. Line 18 holes of two 12-hole patty tins, by pressing small walnut-sized balls of pastry into each hole. Spoon the mincemeat into the pastry shells. Take slightly smaller balls of pastry than before and pat them out between your hands to make round lids, big enough to cover the pies.

STEP 3 Top the pies with their lids, pressing the edges gently together to seal – you don't need to seal them with milk or egg as they will stick on their own. (*The pies may now be frozen for up to 1 month.*) Brush the tops of the pies with the beaten egg. Bake for 20 minutes until golden. Leave to cool in the tin for 5 minutes, then remove to a wire rack. To serve, lightly dust with icing sugar. They will keep for 3–4 days in an airtight container.

Barney Desmazery's
Roly-poly Mince Pies

These pies are more of a Catherine Wheel or Danish in shape, but they have all the essential flavours of a traditional pie. Roll them, slice and then flatten before baking – they're so easy, get your children to give you a hand.

Time: 20 minutes, plus 30 minutes chilling and 30 minutes in the oven

Makes 12 rounds

50g/2oz golden caster sugar

375g pack ready-rolled puff pastry

411g jar traditional mincemeat

1 tbsp milk

25g/1oz flaked almonds

vanilla ice cream, to serve

STEP 1 Preheat the oven to 200°C/Gas 6/fan oven 180°C. Scatter the sugar over the worktop, unroll the pastry and place it on top of the sugar, then roll it out so it's a quarter bigger, but keeps its rectangular shape. Spoon and spread the mincemeat evenly over the pastry leaving a 2cm/¾in border along the longest edges. Fold one of the longest edges over the mincemeat then roll the pastry tightly into a sausage shape while gently pressing the pastry into the mincemeat.

STEP 2 When you get to the other edge, brush it with milk and press down to seal in the mincemeat. Press both ends in gently to plump up the roll and chill for at least 30 minutes to firm. (*The mince pie roll may now be frozen whole or as portioned slices for up to 3 months.*) Cut the roll into 12 rounds, about 3cm/ 1¼in thick.

STEP 3 Lay them evenly spaced on a large baking sheet and flatten them with your hand so they look like squashed Chelsea buns. Scatter the almonds on top and bake for 20–30 minutes until golden brown and the mincemeat sizzles. Leave to cool for 5 minutes – keep them separate so they don't stick together. Eat hot with vanilla ice cream, or just as they are.

James Martin's
Bean and Ham Hock Soup

This recipe combines two inexpensive quality ingredients, peas and ham hocks, for a winning dinner-party first course. Ask your deli for any leftover Serrano ham hocks.

Time: 20 minutes, plus overnight soaking and 2 hours cooking

Serves 6

*Freeze for up to 1 month

200g/8oz dried haricot beans

end piece of ham hock, about 300g/10oz

250ml/9fl oz white wine

1.5 litres/2¾ pints chicken stock

1 onion, finely chopped

3 garlic cloves, finely chopped

¼ leek, finely chopped

½ head of fennel, finely chopped

200g/8oz frozen petit pois

2 tbsp fresh flatleaf parsley, roughly chopped

small handful fresh mint, finely chopped

Maldon sea salt

extra virgin olive oil, for drizzling

1 Soak the haricot beans overnight in plenty of cold water. The next day, drain, then put the beans into a large saucepan with enough cold water to cover. Bring to the boil and boil rapidly for 10 minutes then drain. Put the ham hock in the pan, with the white wine, beans and the stock – everything needs to be just covered with liquid. If not, top up with water. Bring the mixture to the boil, then lower the heat and simmer, uncovered, for about 1½ hours or until the ham starts to fall off the bone.

2 Remove the ham from the stock, set aside and add the onion, garlic, leek and fennel to the stock. Simmer for a further 15 minutes, adding the peas after 5 minutes. Remove all the meat from the ham bone and return it to the soup. *(To freeze at this stage, cool and freeze for up to 1 month.)*

3 Throw the herbs into the soup as well. Season well with salt and pepper and serve drizzled with olive oil.

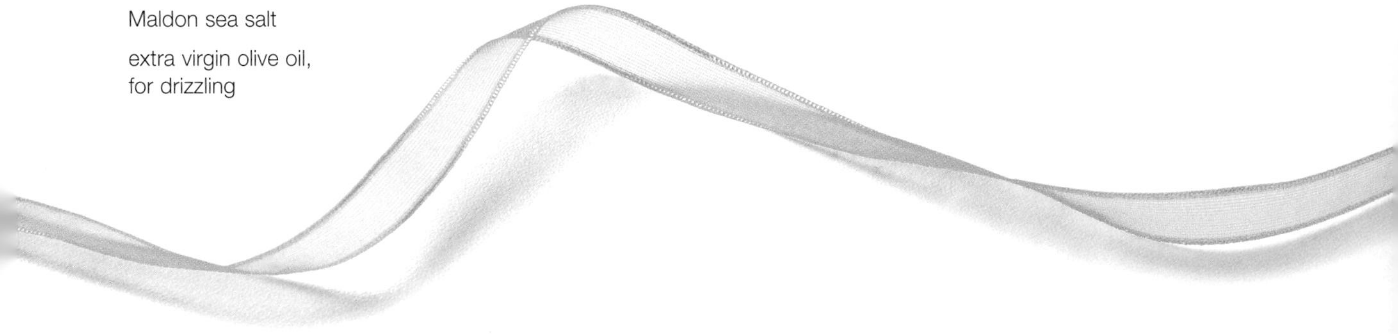

Paul and Jeanne Rankin's
Smoked Mackerel Pâté with Fresh Herbs

A light starter that has a lovely flavour and smooth texture.

Time: 35 minutes, plus 2 hours chilling

Serves 6

*Freeze for up to 1 month

550g/1lb 4oz smoked mackerel fillets

140g/5oz unsalted butter, softened

1 tbsp Dijon mustard

2 tbsp each chopped fresh parsley and dill

2 tbsp snipped fresh chives

1 tbsp small capers, rinsed

4 tbsp lemon juice

¼ tsp cayenne pepper

1 hard-boiled egg yolk

lemon wedges and rocket leaves, to garnish

1 Roughly chop the fish, discarding any skin and bones. Put half the fish and the remaining ingredients in a blender and process until smooth. Taste and season with pepper.

2 Scrape into a bowl and mix in the rest of the fish. Put in a dish.

3 Chill for at least 2 hours, then spoon from the dish. Garnish with lemon and rocket leaves and serve with Irish wheaten or crusty bread.

FREEZE IT
If you are freezing the pâté, double wrap in cling film, label and freeze. Defrost overnight in the fridge and serve as in Step 3.

Silvana Franco's

Champagne and Chicken Liver Pâté

It's well worth setting aside a glass of Champagne or sparkling wine for this recipe. It imparts a unique flavour, and the bubbles give the pâté a very light consistency.

Time: 35–45 minutes, plus overnight chilling

Serves 8

*Freeze for up to 1 month

25g/1oz butter

500g/1lb 2oz chicken livers, thawed if frozen and trimmed if necessary

2 garlic cloves, roughly chopped

142ml carton double cream

125ml/4fl oz Champagne or semi-dry sparkling wine

1 tsp light muscovado sugar

TO SERVE

4 cinnamon and raisin bagels

80g packet wild rocket leaves

truffle oil or extra virgin olive oil

butter, to serve

1 Melt the butter in a frying pan and cook the livers and garlic over a fairly high heat for 5–8 minutes, stirring occasionally, until the livers are browned and caramelised on the outside, but slightly pink in the centre. Allow to cool for 5 minutes.

2 Whizz the chicken livers and all the buttery juices to a paste in a food processor. With the motor running, pour in the cream, followed by the Champagne, until well blended and completely smooth. Season with the sugar, 1 teaspoon salt and plenty of ground black pepper. Pour into a bowl, cover with cling film and chill overnight. The pâté will keep in the fridge for up to 2 days or can be frozen for 1 month.

TO SERVE

1 Heat the grill to high. Cut the bagels into very thin rounds with a serrated knife, then toast them on both sides until pale golden.

2 Using two dessertspoons to get a good shape, scoop the pâté on to eight serving plates, then top with rocket leaves and drizzle over a little oil. Serve with the warm bagel toasts and butter on the side.

Tony Tobin's
Ratatouille with Goats' Cheese and Herby Crumble

This satisfying dish contains so many vegetables that it's a meal itself. It works as a hearty lunch or supper dish for relaxed entertaining. It's also a great non-meat option when you have vegetarian guests around for dinner.

Time: 25 minutes, plus 1–1¼ hours in the oven

Serves 4

*Freeze for up to 2 months

2 aubergines

3 courgettes

2 red peppers

1 green pepper

6 tbsp olive oil

2 onions, coarsely chopped

2 garlic cloves, crushed

400g can Italian chopped tomatoes

a large handful of fresh basil, chopped

350g/12oz goats' cheese with a rind, such as Capricorn, cut into bite-sized chunks

FOR THE CRUMBLE

350g/12oz sliced white bread, crusts removed

1 tbsp green pesto

1 tbsp each chopped fresh parsley, basil and chives

1 Cut the aubergines and courgettes into thick slices, no thinner than 2cm/¾in, then halve the slices across. Set aside. Cut the peppers in half, remove and discard the seeds, then cut the peppers into bite-sized chunks. Set aside.

2 Heat 5 tablespoons of the olive oil in a large pan, add the onions and garlic and gently fry for 8–10 minutes. Add the aubergines, courgettes and peppers and fry for a further 10 minutes. Tip in the chopped tomatoes, season well, cover and cook for 20 minutes. Remove the pan from the heat, stir in the chopped basil and leave aside to cool.

3 Meanwhile, for the crumble, put the bread into a food processor and blend to fine crumbs. Add the pesto, herbs, the remaining olive oil and plenty of seasoning, then blend again.

4 Fold the goats' cheese through the ratatouille. Spoon into a 2 litre/3½ pint ovenproof dish. Sprinkle the herby crumb mixture over the top of the ratatouille.

5 Preheat the oven to 190°C/Gas 5/fan oven 170°C and bake the crumble for 25 minutes until crisp and golden.

FREEZE AHEAD
Follow the recipe to the end of Step 4. Double wrap in its dish in cling film and freeze for up to 2 months. To serve, put the frozen crumble into the fridge to thaw at least 8 hours before you cook it. Continue from Step 5. Or, to save space in your freezer, make the ratatouille up to the end of Step 3 and freeze all the components separately; thaw as above and continue from Step 4.

Tony Tobin's
Pork and Parsnip Cobbler

Pork and apples are a great combination, but add parsnips and apricots into the mix and it becomes a match made in heaven. The herby cobbler topping means this dish needs little or no accompaniment.

Time: 45 minutes, plus 2½ hours in the oven

Serves 8

*Freeze for up to 2 months

6 tbsp vegetable oil

900g/2lb diced pork

2 small onions, finely sliced

1 tbsp plain flour

2 celery sticks, finely chopped

225g/8oz ready-to-eat dried apricots

finely grated zest of 1 lemon

finely grated zest of 1 orange

2 Cox's apples, peeled and chopped

3 garlic cloves, crushed

2 tsp each finely chopped fresh thyme, rosemary and sage

good pinch of curry powder

½ tsp ground fennel seeds

½ bottle red wine

600ml/1 pint vegetable stock

650g/1lb 7oz parsnips

FOR THE COBBLER CRUST

200g/8oz self-raising flour

85g/3oz shredded suet

50g/2oz chilled butter, grated

3 tbsp chopped fresh parsley

finely grated zest and juice of 1 lemon

beaten egg, to glaze

1 For the filling, heat 2 tablespoons of the oil in a large pan and fry the pork in small batches for 4–5 minutes until just browned, then remove with a slotted spoon and set aside. Add the onions to the pan and fry for 5–6 minutes until soft and golden. Return the pork to the pan and sprinkle in the flour. Cook for 1 minute, stirring well.

2 Add the celery, apricots, lemon and orange zest, apples, garlic, herbs and spices. Pour in the wine and stock and bring to simmering point, then cover and gently cook for 1¼ hours or until the pork is tender. Remove from the heat.

3 Meanwhile, preheat the oven to 200°C/Gas 6/fan oven 180°C. Peel and cut the parsnips into 2.5cm/1in dice. Pour the remaining oil into a roasting tin and heat in the oven for 5 minutes. Tip the parsnip chunks into the roasting tin and coat in the hot oil. Roast in the oven for 30 minutes until cooked through and golden brown. Drain and set aside. When the pork is tender, stir in the parsnips. Spoon into a 2 litre/3½ pint ovenproof dish and leave to cool completely.

4 For the cobbler crust, sift the flour and season. Add the suet, butter and parsley and lightly mix in with a fork. Make a well in the centre, then add the lemon zest and juice and gently bring together to make a soft and pliable dough. If it is too dry, add a little cold water, but don't knead the dough or it will become tough. Reduce the temperature to 180°C/Gas 4/fan oven 160°C.

5 Roll out the dough on a lightly floured surface to about 5mm/¼in thick. Cut the dough into rounds using a 7.5cm/3in pastry cutter. Re-roll the trimmings and cut out more rounds until all the dough is used up. Arrange the circles of dough on top of the casserole so that they slightly overlap on top.

6 Brush the dough with beaten egg and bake in the oven for 45 minutes until the crust is golden and lightly puffed.

FREEZE AHEAD
Make the pork and parsnip cobbler up to the end of Step 5. Double wrap in its dish in cling film and freeze for up to 2 months. The evening before serving, put the frozen cobbler in the fridge and leave to thaw overnight. Continue from Step 6.

Paul and Jeanne Rankin's

Daube of Beef with Spiced Beetroot

This one-pot dish is singing with festive flavours. The beetroot gives a wonderfully earthy taste that's just right for cold wintry nights. Serve simply with a creamy mash and a warming glass or two of red wine.

Time: 1 hour, plus overnight marinating and 1½ hours cooking

Serves 6

*Freeze for up to 2 months

1kg/2lb 4oz stewing steak, cut into 5cm/2in cubes

100g/4oz unsmoked streaky bacon, finely chopped

2 carrots, cut into small dice

2 onions, cut into small dice

1 small celery stick, cut into small dice

2 garlic cloves, crushed

½ tsp chopped fresh thyme

1 bay leaf

finely grated zest of 1 orange

350ml/12fl oz port (½ bottle)

2 tbsp vegetable oil

1 tbsp plain flour

250ml/8fl oz beef stock, made from a cube

FOR THE SPICED BEETROOT

500ml/18fl oz red wine

200ml/7fl oz red wine vinegar

140g/5oz dark muscovado sugar

½ tsp fennel seeds, crushed or ground

1 garlic clove, crushed

2.5cm/1in piece fresh root ginger, grated

1 red chilli, seeded and very finely chopped

500g/1lb 2oz cooked beetroot

1 Put the beef, bacon, carrots, onions, celery, garlic, thyme, bay leaf and orange zest into a large shallow bowl. Pour in the port, cover with cling film and leave in the fridge to marinate overnight.

2 Meanwhile, for the beetroot, pour the wine into a saucepan, then add the vinegar, sugar, fennel, garlic, ginger and chilli and bring to the boil. Reduce the heat and simmer for 30 minutes. Cut the beetroot into wedges and put in a large bowl. Pour the hot wine mixture over the beetroot. Allow to cool, then cover and leave in the fridge to marinate overnight.

3 Drain the meat and vegetable mixture, reserving the marinating liquid. Separate the meat from the vegetables as best you can and set the vegetables aside. Heat the oil in a large casserole dish or saucepan and fry the beef pieces in batches over a high heat for 3–4 minutes until just browned. Remove with a slotted spoon and set aside.

4 Add the reserved vegetable mixture to the casserole and cook for 3–4 minutes until the onion is softened. Add the flour and cook for 1 minute, stirring continuously. Return the beef to the pan with the reserved marinade and the stock and season well. Bring to simmering point, cover and gently cook for 1½ hours until the beef is tender.

5 Carefully remove all the beef and vegetables from the pan, using a slotted spoon, and set aside. Drain the marinade from the beetroot and add it to the cooking juices in the pan. Bring to the boil and simmer for 5–6 minutes until the sauce has slightly thickened and has a coating consistency. Return the meat and vegetables to the sauce, then stir in the beetroot. Heat through for 2–3 minutes and serve.

FREEZE AHEAD

Make the recipe up to the end of Step 4. Follow Step 5, but simmer the sauce for only 1–2 minutes instead of 5–6 minutes. Once you have completed Step 5, leave the daube to cool completely and spoon it into a freezerproof container. Cover, label and freeze for up to 2 months. The evening before serving, put the frozen daube into the fridge and leave to thaw overnight. Transfer it back into the casserole or saucepan and reheat slowly on the hob until it is simmering and piping hot.

Moyra Fraser's
Venison in Beer with Drunken Prunes

Making this hearty casserole ahead and freezing it makes for relaxed entertaining around Christmas. Defrost overnight in the fridge, then leave it another day before cooking as the flavours improve. In Scotland, we serve it with bashed neeps (swede) and carrots, cooked until tender then bashed with a potato masher until crushed but not smooth.

Time: 30–40 minutes, plus overnight marinating and 3–3½ hours in the oven

Serves 8

*Freeze for up to 2 months

1.3kg/3lb shoulder of venison or beef, cut into 4cm/1½in pieces

3 garlic cloves, sliced

3 bay leaves

few sprigs of fresh thyme

2–3 pieces dried mushroom, optional

850ml/1½ pints dark stout, such as Mackeson stout, about 3 small cans

300ml/½ pint port

200g/8oz ready-to-eat dried prunes, pitted

2 tbsp balsamic vinegar

50g/2oz butter

4 tbsp olive oil

225g/8oz smoked back bacon, cut into thin strips

900g/2lb shallots, peeled and left whole

2 celery sticks, finely chopped

450g/1lb medium-sized mushrooms such as chestnut, halved if large

4 tsp plain flour

ONE OR TWO DAYS BEFORE

1 Put the meat in a large non-metallic bowl with the garlic, bay leaves, thyme and dried mushrooms, if using. Pour in the stout and 200ml/7fl oz of the port, cover and leave to marinate in the fridge overnight, or until needed.

2 Put the prunes in a small bowl and pour in the balsamic vinegar and the remaining port. Cover and leave to soak overnight at cool room temperature.

ON THE DAY

3 Preheat the oven to 150°C/Gas 2/fan oven 130°C. Drain the meat, reserving all the marinade. Pat the meat dry. Heat the butter and oil in a large flameproof casserole. On a high heat, brown the meat in batches until dark brown. Remove the meat and keep warm. Should the fat burn, pour it away, wipe out the pan and add a little more oil and butter.

4 Add the bacon, shallots and celery to the casserole and fry until golden. Stir in the mushrooms and fry, stirring, for 2–3 minutes. Stir in the flour until blended, add the meat and reserved marinade.

5 Bring to a steady boil then cover with a tight-fitting lid and cook in the oven for 2½–3 hours or until very tender.

6 Add the prunes and their soaking liquid and cook for a further 30 minutes.

FREEZE AHEAD

Cool, then spoon into a freezerproof container. When cold, freeze for up to 2 months.

Phil Vickery's
Chocolate Torte

Torte is the German word for a cake with layers of sponge, cream and meringue. The lavishness varies, but I've kept my recipe to three simple scrumptious rich and exceedingly naughty levels. The perfect Christmas treat.

Time: 30–40 minutes, plus overnight freezing and 20 minutes in the oven

Cuts into 8 slices

*Freeze for up to 2 months

FOR THE SPONGE

3 medium eggs

100g/4oz golden caster sugar

85g/3oz plain flour, sifted

2 tsp good quality cocoa powder

3–4 tbsp chocolate liqueur or brandy

FOR THE FILLING

280g/10oz good quality bitter chocolate (70% cocoa), broken into pieces

275g sachet Supercook Whisk & Bake Meringue mix

175ml/6fl oz double cream, lightly whipped

FOR THE GLAZE

250ml/9fl oz double cream

½ tsp good quality cocoa powder

200g/8oz good quality bitter chocolate, very finely chopped

bought chocolate truffles, to decorate

1 Preheat the oven to 180°C/Gas 4/fan oven 160°C. Lightly grease the base of a 23cm/9in round spring-form cake tin and line with greaseproof paper. Put the eggs and sugar in a large bowl and whisk with an electric hand whisk until the mixture leaves a very thick trail. Carefully fold in the flour and cocoa using a large metal spoon. Pour the mixture into the prepared cake tin and bake for 20 minutes or until well risen and springy to the touch. Cool slightly.

2 Run a sharp knife around the edge of the cake, then remove the sides of the tin. Cool the cake completely.

3 Remove the sponge from the bottom of the tin. Wash the tin, re-assemble, then line the base and sides with clear acetate (file sleeves are good). Invert the sponge and return to the lined tin. Sprinkle with chocolate liqueur or brandy.

4 For the filling, melt the chocolate in a bowl set over a pan of simmering water. Allow to cool slightly while you whisk the meringue mix until thick and glossy. Carefully fold the chocolate into the meringue and then fold in the whipped cream, but do not overbeat. Spoon into the tin, level the surface, cover with cling film and freeze overnight.

5 Meanwhile, make the glaze. Put the double cream and cocoa powder into a saucepan and bring to the boil. Place the chocolate in a large bowl and add the hot cream mixture, whisking well until the chocolate has melted and thickened. Cool slightly, then pour this over the top of the cake to cover completely.

6 Chill for 15–20 minutes until the glaze has set, then you can open the clip on the spring-form tin. Remove the tin and discard the cling film. Transfer the torte to a serving plate. Decorate with truffles. Alternatively, decorate with chocolate shavings made by running a potato peeler along the flat side of a slightly softened bar of chocoalate. For easy slicing, cut the torte with a hot, wet knife.

FREEZE AHEAD

Make as above. Freeze undecorated in the tin for 4–5 hours or overnight, then overwrap in foil and label. Freeze for up to 2 months. To serve, remove from freezer and leave at room temperature for 30–40 minutes to thaw slightly. Remove from the tin and decorate with truffles or chocolate shavings.

Phil Vickery's
Frutti Ice Cream Cake

This ice-cream terrine makes a stunning centrepiece for any festive table. Its professional look belies how easy it is to make. Take this impressive dessert to the table for your guests to admire before cutting into it.

Time: 30-40 minutes, plus overnight soaking, overnight freezing and 15 minutes in the oven

Makes 12 slices

*Freeze for up to 3 months

140g/5oz sultanas, currants and natural dyed cherries

85g/3oz candied mixed fruit peel, chopped

4–5 tbsp brandy

3 medium eggs

100g/4oz golden caster sugar

100g/4oz plain flour

½ tsp ground nutmeg

½ tsp mixed spice

500ml tub vanilla ice cream

500ml tub cherry or other fruit ice cream

icing sugar, to decorate

1 Preheat the oven to 190°C/Gas 5/fan oven 170°C. Soak the fruits in the brandy overnight.

2 Line a 39 x 29cm/15½ x 11½in Swiss roll tin with baking parchment and lightly grease. Whisk the eggs and sugar in an electric mixer until thick and the mixture leaves a trail. Carefully fold in the flour and spices. Spread the mixture into the tin and bake for 15 minutes until well risen and springy to touch. Turn out on to a wire rack and remove the lining paper.

3 Take the vanilla ice cream out of the freezer to soften for 15 minutes. Trim the edges of the sponge. Place a 1.3kg/3lb (30cm/12in long) loaf tin rim-side down along one of the short ends of the sponge and cut around (this will become the terrine base). Trim the remaining sponge to give a rectangle of about 23 x 29cm/9 x 11½in. Remove the soaked fruit with a slotted spoon and fold into the vanilla ice cream. Sprinkle any leftover brandy over the sponge. Place a rectangle of sponge in the tin, with the browned side facing outwards. Press into the tin to line the base and two long sides.

4 Spoon the cherry ice cream into the base of the sponge-lined tin. Level the surface and freeze for 20 minutes. Spoon over the vanilla and fruit ice cream and level the surface. Top with the reserved strip of sponge. Press down lightly and wrap the whole tin tightly in cling film. Freeze overnight.

5 To serve, soften slightly in the fridge, then dust with icing sugar to decorate.

FREEZE AHEAD

Make the ice cream cake to the end of Step 4. Open-freeze in the tin for 4–5 hours or overnight until solid, then overwrap in foil, label and freeze for up to 3 months. To serve, remove from the freezer and leave at room temperature for 20–25 minutes to thaw slightly. Remove from the tin and dust lightly with icing sugar to decorate.

CHAPTER 2

Easy Entertaining

We all love inviting people over at Christmas, but often the idea is better than the reality. No one wants to be in the kitchen when everyone else is having fun.

It's also easy to get things out of proportion – you either end up cooking too much and have a fridge full of leftovers or don't make enough and people go home feeling hungry.

To take the guesswork out of party entertaining, turn to our three prepare-ahead menus, which mean you will be mingling rather than making food on the night.

My prepare-ahead supper (page 42) makes an excellent Christmas Eve or Boxing Day menu as there isn't a scrap of turkey in sight. The easiest option is to lay out the food buffet-style for everyone to help themselves.

If you're having a really **informal gathering**, with people dropping in over the course of an evening, then opt for **canapés** that can be handed round on platters. We've created two collections. You don't have to make them all, just pick and mix your favourites, then calculate how many you'll need depending on the numbers you've invited.

These recipes are all straightforward. Some are **so simple**, you can even make more during the evening. Others like the Stilton and Poppy Seed Sablés (page 54) can be frozen ahead in batches and defrosted the night before.

But don't feel everything has to be home-made, supplement your nibbles with a few bought canapés, crudités and dips, and if you're worried about people going hungry, have crusty breads and cheese in reserve.

A selection of welcoming festive drinks will also get everyone in a party mood. **Mulled wine** is a must and can be simmering on the gentlest heat, while you make the other drinks. If you don't want to dust down the cocktail shaker, offer flutes of Italian sparkling wine (Prosecco) topped up with peach liqueur for a Bellini, or Champagne or sparkling wine with cranberry juice and a few frozen cranberries.

Whatever you decide to make, we can guarantee these recipes won't let you down.

Mary Cadogan's
Prepare-ahead supper

This menu makes an excellent Boxing Day buffet when everyone is turkeyed out. It's full of lively and exotic flavours. You can prepare it ahead of time and chill, or even freeze, the lamb and dessert. All that's required on the night is a little light garnishing.

On the menu

Serves 6–8

* Prawn and Avocado Escabèche with Crisp Lettuce and Poppadums

* Malaysian Spiced Lamb with Coconut and Mint

* Crunchy Cucumber and Carrot Salad

* Cranberry and Pistachio Rice

* Sparkling Lemon and Amaretti Ice

Prawn and Avocado Escabèche

Guests will welcome this light dish as it's incredibly refreshing and it won't break the calorie bank.

Time: 20–30 minutes

Serves 6–8

juice of 3 limes

5 spring onions, thinly sliced

1 tbsp tomato paste

large pinch of dried oregano

300g/10oz ripe tomatoes, cherry or plum, finely chopped

1 green chilli, seeded and finely chopped

400g bag large frozen, cooked, peeled prawns

2 ripe avocados

3 tbsp chopped fresh coriander

iceberg lettuce leaves and ready-cooked poppadums, to serve

1 In a non-metallic bowl, mix the lime juice, spring onions, tomato paste, oregano, tomatoes and chilli. Mix well, season with salt and pepper, then cover with cling film. *(This mixture can now be kept in the fridge for up to 3 days.)*

2 Defrost the prawns and pat dry with kitchen paper. Just before serving, peel and cube the avocados. Add to the sauce with the prawns and coriander and mix well. *(This can be done up to 3 hours ahead.)*

3 Carefully separate the lettuce leaves and arrange them over a serving platter. Spoon the prawns and sauce into the cup-shaped leaves and serve with crisp and warmed ready-cooked poppadums.

POPPADUMS MADE EASY
You can buy ready-made poppadums in packs of eight from most major supermarkets. They don't need to be fried or grilled, but just heated in the microwave. You'll need two packs for this recipe.

Malaysian Spiced Lamb with Coconut and Mint

You can substitute 1kg/2.2lb cooked leftover turkey, cut into cubes, for the lamb if you prefer. In that case, the dish only needs simmering for 10 minutes.

Time: 1 hour, plus
1½ hours simmering

Serves 6–8

*Freeze for up to 3 months

6 cardamom pods

1 tsp cumin seeds

½–1 tsp chilli flakes

2 tbsp ground coriander

1 tbsp paprika

3 onions

3 garlic cloves, roughly chopped

5cm/2in piece fresh root ginger, roughly chopped

3 tbsp vegetable oil

1.3kg/3lb boneless lamb, either leg or shoulder, cut into forkable chunks

1 cinnamon stick

1 star anise

400ml can coconut milk

good handful fresh mint leaves, stripped from their stalks, roughly chopped

1 Split the cardamom pods and extract the seeds. Roughly crush the cumin seeds and chilli flakes using a pestle and mortar, then stir in the coriander and paprika.

2 Roughly chop two of the onions. Process in a food processor or blender with the garlic and ginger to form a rough paste. Add the spices, including the cardomom seeds, mix briefly until evenly coloured, then tip into a bowl. Slice the remaining onion. Heat the oil in a pan, add the sliced onion and cook for 5 minutes, until lightly coloured. Add the spice paste and cook gently, stirring, for 5 minutes until it has darkened slightly.

3 Add the lamb to the pan and stir well to coat the pieces in the spice paste. Pour in 425ml/¾ pint water, add the cinnamon and star anise and bring to the boil. Add plenty of salt and pepper, cover tightly and simmer for 1½ hours until the lamb is meltingly tender. Remove the lid for the last half an hour, to reduce and thicken the liquid slightly. *(At this point the dish can be cooled and either stored in the fridge for up to 3 days or frozen for up to 3 months.)*

4 Stir in the coconut milk and simmer for 5 minutes. Taste, adding more salt if needed. Stir in the mint.

Crunchy Cucumber and Carrot Salad

This low-fat dish is another winner at this indulgent time of year.

Time: 20–25 minutes
Serves 6–8
1 cucumber
4 large carrots
1 small red onion, halved and thinly sliced
2 tbsp golden caster sugar
6 tbsp white wine vinegar
1 red chilli, seeded and finely chopped
bunch radishes, sliced

1 Cut the cucumber into three equal chunks, then cut each chunk in half lengthways and slice thinly lengthways. Cut the carrots into ribbons using a potato peeler or mandolin.

2 Put the cucumber and onion in a colander and sprinkle with salt. Leave for 1 hour, rinse and pat dry with kitchen paper.

3 Heat the sugar and vinegar gently in a pan to dissolve the sugar. Stir in the chilli and leave to cool.

4 Tip the vegetables into a serving bowl and drizzle over the dressing, tossing lightly with a little salt and pepper. *(It can now be covered and stored in the fridge for up to 2 hours. Toss again before serving.)*

Cranberry and Pistachio Rice

You'll find the dried cranberries for this recipe alongside the nuts at most major supermarkets. They are sweeter than fresh as the sugar has been concentrated, and they have a pleasant chewy texture.

Time: 20–25 minutes
Serves 6–8
500g/1lb 2oz basmati rice
pinch of saffron strands
100g/4oz dried cranberries or sour cherries
50g/2oz shelled pistachios, chopped

1 Rinse the rice several times, then tip into a pan with 1.2 litres/2 pints water, the saffron, cranberries and 1 teaspoon salt. Bring to the boil, stir once, cover and simmer for 12 minutes, until the rice is tender and the water is absorbed.

2 Tip into a serving bowl and scatter the pistachios on top.

Sparkling Lemon and Amaretti Ice

This creamy dessert can be frozen complete with its topping, leaving you very little to do on the day itself.

Time: 30–45 minutes, plus a minimum of 4 hours in the freezer

Serves 6–8

* Freeze for up to 2 months

140g/5oz amaretti biscuits

50g/2oz butter, melted

2 x 250g tubs ricotta or curd cheese

175g/6oz golden caster sugar

grated zest and juice of 2 lemons

284ml carton double cream

FOR THE TOPPING

2 lemons, very thinly sliced

85g/3oz golden caster sugar

1 Line the base and sides of a 20cm/8in cake tin with a round and two or three strips of plastic cut from two A4 clear, unused plastic folders. Crush the amaretti biscuits fairly finely and mix into the melted butter, stirring well. Press into the base of the tin, smoothing with the back of a metal spoon.

2 Tip the cheese into a large bowl, beat briefly to soften, then beat in the sugar, lemon zest and juice. Whip the cream until it just holds its shape, then fold into the mixture. Pour the lemon mixture into the tin and smooth the top. Freeze for 4 hours.

3 Put the lemon slices in a pan, cover with water and bring to the boil, reduce the heat and simmer for 20 minutes. Drain well.

4 Tip the sugar into a small pan and add 3 tablespoons water. Heat gently to melt the sugar, then add the lemon slices, increase the heat and cook until the lemons are caramelised (about 4–5 minutes). Cool to room temperature, then arrange in overlapping circles over the top of the dessert. Drizzle over any syrup, then return to the freezer. *(Can be frozen for up to 2 months at this point.)*

5 Remove the dessert from the freezer 2–3 hours before serving, peel off the plastic and set on a serving plate. *(Timing is not too critical, as it won't collapse, it just becomes softer.)* Store in the fridge until you are ready to serve.

FLAVOUR VARIATION

You could make this dessert with clementines instead.
Replace the lemons with 2 large clementines and add 3 tablespoons of mandarin liqueur to the cheesecake mixture instead of the juice of 2 lemons.

Celebration canapés

Make big batches of these bites and you'll be well prepared for celebrating Christmas in style. Some you can prepare ahead, others you can freeze, so they're great for last-minute drinks celebrations. All taste divine and look so much more appetising than anything you can buy. They also require the minimum of cooking skill as the chefs and cooks have put all the hard work into making sure they're straightforward, but sensational.

On the menu

Serves 6–8

* Chicory and Houmous Bites

* Red Pepper and Houmous Bites

* Crunchy Christmas Crostini

* Spicy Prawn Poppadums

* Satay Shots

* Rosemary and Cheese Straws

* Lamb Koftas with Spicy Dipping Sauce

* Stilton and Poppy Seed Sablés

* Artichoke and Mint Dip

Sara Buenfeld's
Chicory and Houmous Bites

Chicory leaves make a great base for these simple canapés, which are filled with bought houmous. Make these and the red pepper bites for the most festive-looking platter.

Time: 15–20 minutes

Makes 16–18 (allow 3–4 per guest)

2 large heads of chicory

1 carrot

175g tub houmous

16–18 black olives, preferably pitted

1 Up to 2 hours ahead separate the chicory into boat-shaped leaves, and trim the ends so that they are all roughly the same size. You will probably get about eight or nine decent-sized leaves from each head of chicory. As the leaves get closer to the heart of the chicory, they will be too small to use for canapés, so save these to add to wintry salads.

2 Peel the carrot, then keep peeling off strips until you have as many as the number of chicory leaves.

3 Drop spoonfuls of houmous on to the chicory, then add a carrot curl and an olive to each. They'll keep fresh in the fridge for about 2 hours.

RED PEPPER AND HOUMOUS VARIATION

Make as before, using 2 heads of red chicory. Top with 175g tub roasted red pepper houmous then scatter with chopped toasted pecans – you will need about 20. Dust lightly with paprika to serve, but don't go mad, as it's quite peppery.

Barney Desmazery's
Crunchy Christmas Crostini

The tanginess of the beetroot pickle goes well with the Stilton, but you can use other chutneys or pickles if you prefer.

Time: 25–35 minutes

Makes 25 (allow 3–4 per guest)

1 ready-to-bake ciabatta loaf

1 tbsp olive oil

1 large wedge Stilton, about 200g/8oz

about half a 290g jar salad beetroot pickle

handful of celery leaves taken from the middle of a head of celery

1 Up to a day ahead, preheat the oven to 200°C/Gas 6/fan oven 180°C. Slice the ciabatta into about 25 thin slices. Lay them on a couple of baking trays and brush with the oil. Toast in the oven for 10 minutes until they begin to go golden, checking after 5 minutes as the trays may need turning. Store in an airtight tin until ready to use.

2 Up to an hour ahead cut the Stilton into slices a little smaller than the toasts (this is easier to do if the cheese is cold from the fridge), and keep covered.

3 Just before serving preheat the oven to 200°C/Gas 6/fan oven 180°C. Spoon a little pile of beetroot on to the end of each piece of bread. Prop a slice of cheese up against each pile of beetroot and bake for 3–4 minutes until the cheese starts to melt. You don't want it too melty – try to catch it just as it's starting to ooze over the edge. Top each cheesy canapé with a little sprig of celery leaves and serve immediately.

Angela Nilsen's
Spicy Prawn Poppadums

These must be the quickest canapés to prepare. Make them to order as they will soften if left to stand too long.

Time: 10–15 minutes

Makes 24 (allow 3–4 per guest)

24 cooked and peeled extra large tiger prawns, thawed if frozen

24 ready-to-eat mini poppadums, plain or assorted

200g tub tzatziki (Total is nice and thick)

chopped fresh coriander

paprika, for dusting

1 Up to 2 hours ahead dry the prawns on kitchen paper and keep covered in the fridge. Lay out the poppadums on a serving platter.

2 Just before serving, spoon a little tzatziki into each poppadum. Stand a prawn on top, then finish with a scattering of coriander and a light dusting of paprika.

Jeni Wright's
Satay Shots

Guests can't fail to be impressed when you hand around these shot glasses filled with a warm spicy sauce and mini chicken satay sticks.

Time: 20–30 minutes

Makes 36 (allow around 3 per guest)

4 skinless boneless chicken breasts

3 tbsp soy sauce

1 heaped tbsp Very Lazy Chillies (available at supermarkets) or chilli paste

2 garlic cloves, crushed

1 tbsp vegetable oil

1 heaped tbsp light muscovado sugar

1 lime, cut in half

415g jar ready-made satay sauce (Sharwood's Indonesian Satay Sauce is good)

12 lime slices

1 Up to a day ahead cut the chicken breasts into 36 thin strips and put them in a dish with the soy sauce, chillies or chilli paste, garlic, oil and sugar. Mix together until the chicken is coated, then thread each strip on to a bamboo skewer. Line the skewers up on a baking tray and keep covered in the fridge until ready to cook.

2 Before serving, preheat the oven to 190°C/Gas 5/fan oven 170°C. Put the tray in the hottest part of the oven for 10 minutes. Meanwhile, warm the satay sauce in a pan, then spoon a little into each of 12 shot glasses or small tumblers.

3 When the chicken is done, remove the tray from the oven and squeeze over the lime juice. Pop 3 skewers into each shot glass and ease a slice of lime on to each rim. Serve warm or cold – they're nice either way.

Henry Harris's
Rosemary and Cheese Straws

These cheese straws are meltingly gorgeous and give a lovely rosemary and cheese hit. Make batches for the freezer as they can be cooked straight from frozen.

Time: 40–45 minutes

Makes 36 (allow 6 per guest)

* Freeze for up to 2 months

2 egg yolks

2 tsp Dijon or wholegrain mustard

375g pack ready-rolled puff pastry

3 tbsp roughly chopped fresh rosemary leaves, plus extra for sprinkling

100g/4oz gruyère or emmental, finely grated

2 tbsp finely grated Parmesan

sea salt, for sprinkling

1 Preheat the oven to 200°C/Gas 6/fan oven 180°C. Mix 1 egg yolk and the mustard in a bowl and stir until smooth. Set aside.

2 Lightly flour the worksurface and unroll the pastry. Prick all over with a fork. Brush the egg and mustard mixture over the pastry.

3 Evenly sprinkle the 3 tablespoons of rosemary and the cheeses over the pastry and lightly press into the pastry. Cut the pastry in half lengthways, then cut each length widthways into 2cm/¾in wide strips. Twist the strips to look like barley sugar twists.

4 Space out on two large non-stick or parchment-lined baking trays. Press both ends of each twist on to the tray. Beat the reserved yolk with 1 teaspoon water and brush over the twists. Sprinkle with the extra rosemary and sea salt. Bake for 12–15 minutes or until puffed and golden. Transfer to a wire rack while still warm.

FREEZING AHEAD
Make the straws up to the end of Step 3. Arrange on a large baking tray and freeze, uncovered, until solid. Pack into a freezerproof box, then label and seal. Freeze for up to 2 months. To serve, remove from the freezer, finish as for Step 4 and bake from frozen for 12–15 minutes.

Henry Harris's
Lamb Koftas with Spicy Dipping Sauce

Serve these hot or at room temperature. The dipping sauce is also good with steak or other meats.

Time: 25–30 minutes

Makes 20 (allow 3 per guest)

* Freeze for up to 2 months

500g/1lb 2oz lean minced lamb

finely grated zest 1 lemon

finely grated zest 1 orange

1 garlic clove, crushed

¼ tsp ground cumin

large handful fresh coriander, finely chopped

large handful fresh mint, finely chopped

1 tsp harissa (find it in the spice and sauces section in supermarkets)

olive oil, for shallow frying

FOR THE DIPPING SAUCE

250ml carton natural yogurt

1 tbsp harissa

squeeze of lemon juice

2 tbsp chopped fresh mint

1 Put all the kofta ingredients, except the oil, into a large bowl. Season and mix well. Shape into 20 small balls. Slightly flatten to prevent rolling while cooking.

2 Heat the oil in a frying pan and fry half the balls for 2 minutes each side. Remove from the pan and drain on kitchen paper. Repeat with the remaining half.

3 Meanwhile, mix together all the dipping sauce ingredients and season. Arrange the kofta balls, some on cocktail sticks, in a bowl and serve with the sauce.

FREEZE AHEAD
Make the kofta balls as in Step 1. Put on a baking tray and freeze, uncovered, until solid. Pack into a freezer bag or freezerproof box and freeze for up to 2 months. Thaw in the fridge for 3–4 hours, cook as for Step 2 and serve with the sauce.

Barney Desmarzery's
Stilton and Poppy Seed Sablés

The polenta in these biscuits makes them wonderfully crumbly, and there's always Stilton to use up at this time of year. They're great served with a crisp glass of white wine.

Time: 30 minutes, plus
1 hour chilling

Makes about 30 biscuits

* Freeze for up to 1 month unbaked

100g/4oz plain flour

85g/3oz cold butter, diced

small pinch of mustard powder

small pinch of cayenne pepper

1 tbsp polenta (this is optional but does add extra crunchiness)

1 tbsp poppy seeds

100g/4oz Stilton, crumbled (it's easier to use if taken straight from the fridge) plus extra, to top the biscuits

1 In a large bowl, rub together the flour, butter, mustard powder, cayenne, polenta, if using, poppy seeds, Stilton and a pinch of salt, using your fingers and hands, until the mixture forms a pastry dough. Knead the dough briefly until it really sticks together and is very lightly speckled with tiny bits of cheese. You can be quite heavy-handed.

2 On a lightly floured surface, roll the dough into a sausage shape with your hands, about 25cm/10in long and 4cm/1½in in diameter, then wrap in cling film and chill for at least 1 hour. *(The pastry can now be chilled for up to 1 week or frozen for up to 1 month. The pastry can be sliced and cooked from frozen but you need to cut it slightly thicker.)*

3 To bake the biscuits, preheat the oven to 190°C/Gas 5/fan oven 170°C. Slice the dough into rounds just under 1cm/½in thick. Lay the rounds a couple of centimetres apart on a baking sheet (or two, if you are cooking all the biscuits at the same time). Put a very small piece of Stilton in the middle of each biscuit, then bake for 10–15 minutes, until the edges are starting to go golden and the cheese is bubbling. Leave to cool slightly before serving. The biscuits will keep for 2–3 days in an airtight tin.

Mary Cadogan's
Artichoke and Mint Dip

All you need is a jar of artichokes in your storecupboard and you can whip up this delicious dip in no time.

Time: 15–20 minutes

Serves 6–8

285g jar artichoke antipasto in oil

a good handful fresh mint leaves, stripped from the stalks

3 tbsp crème fraîche

1–2 tsp lemon juice

6 pitta breads

2 tbsp olive oil

lemon wedge and mint sprig, to garnish

1 Up to a day ahead blitz the artichokes and their oil with the mint in a food processor until fairly smooth. Add the crème fraîche, season and briefly pulse, then add the lemon juice to taste. Tip into a small bowl, cover and chill.

2 Just before serving, preheat the oven to 200°C/Gas 6/fan oven 180°C. Tear the pittas into rough pieces and spread over a couple of baking sheets. Drizzle with olive oil and scatter over some sea salt. Bake for 7–10 minutes until crisp.

3 Set the bowl of dip on a large platter and stick a lemon wedge and a sprig of mint in. Surround with the crisp pitta pieces.

Lorna Brash's Festive drinks

Christmas is the time of year when we have the best array of drinks ingredients to transform into celebration cocktails. This selection of drinks by Lorna Brash will kickstart any get-together, and she's even thoughtfully included a Bloody Mary for the morning after...

Mulled wine (pictured opposite)

Time: 10 minutes, plus standing

Serves 10

115g/4oz caster sugar

4 cloves

1 cinnamon stick

1 orange, sliced

2 lemons, sliced

70cl bottle hearty red wine (Burgundy or claret)

star anise, berries and apple slices, to decorate, optional

1 Put 300ml/½ pint water into a large pan with the sugar, cloves, cinnamon, orange and lemon slices. Heat, stirring occasionally, until the sugar has dissolved. Remove from the heat and leave to infuse for 10–15 minutes. Add the red wine and warm through, taking care not to let the mixture boil. Pour into a jug or punch bowl and decorate with the star anise, berries and apple slices, if liked. Serve warm in heatproof glasses.

Bloody Mary

Time: 5 minutes

Serves 6

250ml/9fl oz vodka

1 litre/1¾ pints vegetable or tomato juice

4 tbsp freshly squeezed lime juice

1 tbsp Tabasco sauce

6 tbsp Worcestershire sauce

lemon slices and celery sticks, to serve

1 Mix all the ingredients together and serve in glasses with plenty of ice. Add lemon slices and a celery stick 'stirrer' to serve.

Cognac fizz

Time: 5 minutes, plus chilling

Serves 8 long/16 short drinks

75cl bottle dry white wine

150ml/¼ pint cognac

150ml/¼ pint Earl Grey tea, cooled

50ml/2fl oz fresh lemon juice

75cl bottle sweet Asti Spumante

1 Mix together the white wine, cognac, Earl Grey tea and lemon juice, then chill until ready to serve. Pour the drink into tall glasses and top up with an equal volume of Asti Spumante.

Caribbean smoothie

Time: 5 minutes, plus chilling

Serves 12

850g can mango pulp

400g can coconut milk

250ml/9fl oz milk

9 tbsp dark rum

1.3 litres/2¼ pints ginger beer

dusting of ground cinnamon, to serve

1 Whisk together the mango pulp, coconut milk, milk and rum, then chill until ready to use. Pour into glasses and add an equal volume of ginger beer to serve. Dust with cinnamon, if liked.

OR TRY THIS ...

Leave out the rum and add a scoop of ice cream to make a fun drink for kids. Reserve a little coconut milk to make ice cubes. Pour the milk into an ice-cube tray, add a few mint leaves, then freeze. Put a few of the cubes in each glass and pour over the smoothie.

Merilees Parker's
Last-minute drinks party

These speedy, spur-of-the-moment canapés are ideal for an impromptu drinks party. Decide to have friends around in the morning and by suppertime, you'll have an amazing array of food. None of these recipes takes longer than half an hour to make, then you can just pop them in the oven. Most can also be partly made ahead, which is highlighted in the recipe.

On the menu

❋ Glazed Honey and Mustard Sausages

❋ Crispy Potato Skins with Creamy Chive Dip

❋ Hoisin Chicken in Crisp Lettuce

❋ Pear and Gorgonzola Crostini

❋ Prosciutto and Rocket Rolls

❋ Party Punch

Glazed Honey and Mustard Sausages

Most supermarkets have a good selection of mini sausages at Christmas, so you're certain to find something tasty.

Time: 15 minutes, plus 30–35 minutes in the oven

Serves 8–12

2 tbsp sunflower oil

48 cocktail sausages, separated if linked

3 tbsp clear honey

3 tbsp wholegrain or Dijon mustard

ketchup and mustard, to serve

1 Preheat the oven to 200°C/Gas 6/fan oven 180°C. Pour the oil into a large roasting tin and heat in the oven for 3–4 minutes. Tip the sausages into the roasting tin and toss to lightly coat in the oil. Roast for 20–25 minutes or until browned and cooked through.
2 Drain the sausages well on kitchen paper, then tip them into a clean roasting tin. Blend the honey and mustard together in a small bowl, pour over the sausages and stir and shake them so they become coated. Return to the oven for 5 minutes, turning them over halfway. Serve hot or warm, with cocktail sticks and little pots of ketchup and mustard for dipping.

PREPARE AHEAD
You can roast the sausages the day before, cool them on kitchen paper, then keep in a plastic container in the fridge overnight. Toss in the honey and mustard mix and reheat for 10–12 minutes in the oven before serving. Alternatively, heat half the sausages through in half the honey and mustard mix just before your party, then do the other half just as the first batch runs out.

Crispy Potato Skins with Creamy Chive Dip

These are a real party pleaser – tasty, warming and satisfying.

Time: 20 minutes, plus
1½ hours in the oven

Serves 8–12

6 baking potatoes

5 tbsp olive oil

284ml tub soured cream

3 tbsp creamed horseradish

4 tbsp snipped fresh chives

a few chive stems, to
garnish

PREPARE AHEAD

**Bake the potatoes and
make and chill the dip the
day before. Two hours
before your party, prepare
the potatoes from Step 2
and put in the oven
30 minutes before your
guests arrive.
Alternatively, roast the
potatoes in two batches –
half before the party
starts and half when
these have been eaten.**

1 Preheat the oven to 200°C/Gas 6/fan oven 180°C. Roughly prick the potatoes all over with a fork and bake in the oven for about 1 hour or until tender.

2 Remove from the oven, leave until cool enough to handle, then cut each potato into eight wedges and put in a large bowl with the olive oil. Season generously. Mix well, making sure that each wedge is well coated with oil and seasoning.

3 Stand the potato wedges on a large non-stick baking sheet and roast in the oven for 20–30 minutes or until really crispy and golden. Meanwhile, mix the soured cream in a serving bowl with the horseradish and snipped chives.

4 Serve the wedges straight from the oven, with the soured cream dip and garnished with the chives.

Hoisin Chicken in Crisp Lettuce

If you can't find Little Gem lettuce, use iceberg or chicory leaves instead as edible containers for this delectable oriental-style chicken filling.

Time: 40 minutes

Serves 8–12

1 tbsp dry sherry

1 tsp cornflour

1 tbsp light soy sauce

2 tbsp hoisin sauce

½ tsp sugar

5 tbsp chicken stock

1 tbsp sunflower oil

1 large garlic clove, crushed

3 spring onions, chopped, green separated from white, plus 1 shredded to garnish

200g/8oz minced chicken

220g can water chestnuts, drained and chopped

2–4 tbsp chopped fresh coriander

3 Little Gem lettuces, each broken into 8 individual leaves

1 In a bowl, mix the sherry and cornflour to a smooth liquid. Add the soy and hoisin sauces, sugar and stock. Set aside.

2 Heat the oil in a wok or large frying pan, toss in the garlic and whites of the spring onions and stir fry for 2–3 minutes. Tip in the chicken and stir fry over a high heat until it colours, using the back of a spoon to break up any big lumps. Tip in the water chestnuts and stir fry for a further 1–2 minutes.

3 Push the chicken mixture to one side of the wok. Pour the sherry mixture into the empty part and stir for 1–2 minutes until it bubbles and thickens. Combine thoroughly, then leave to simmer for 5–10 minutes. Season and stir in the green part of the spring onions and coriander.

4 Lay the lettuce leaves on serving plates, spoon in the warm mixture without overfilling, and scatter with the shredded spring onion. Suggest your guests roll the lettuce up around the filling to make a shape that's easy to eat as finger food.

PREPARE AHEAD

You can cook the filling the day before, leave to cool and store in a plastic container in the fridge overnight. Reheat it well for 5–10 minutes until hot, stirring all the time and adding a splash of hot water if it's too dry. Alternatively, make up half the lettuce boats just before the party, and keep the remaining chicken mix warm until you are ready to use it. Get the remaining lettuce boats ready on a serving platter before the party starts so all you have to do is spoon in the filling.

Pear and Gorgonzola Crostini

Choose firm pears for this recipe, otherwise they'll break up when poached.

Time: 40–45 minutes

Serves 8–12

2 small firm pears, unpeeled

2 tbsp clear honey

150ml/¼ pint port

150ml/¼ pint red wine

1 French bâton or baguette (30cm/12in long)

2 tbsp extra virgin olive oil

200g/8oz gorgonzola, at room temperature

mustard and cress, to garnish

1 Halve and core the pears, then cut each one into 12 small wedges. Place in a heavy-based saucepan with the honey, port and wine. Cook for 5–10 minutes or until the pears are just tender when pierced with the tip of a sharp knife (they shouldn't be soft).

2 Carefully tip the pears into a sieve set over a small saucepan and allow them to drain thoroughly.

3 Reduce the liquid in the saucepan by two-thirds – it should have a syrupy consistency like runny honey. This will take 10–12 minutes. Pour the syrup into a small bowl and allow to cool while you prepare the crostini.

4 Preheat the grill to hot. Cut the bread into 24 slices and brush both sides of each slice with olive oil. Grill until the crostini are golden on both sides. This only takes a minute, so keep watch.

5 Spread each crostini with a little gorgonzola and top with a poached pear wedge. Arrange the crostini on a serving plate and drizzle with the port syrup using a teaspoon. Sprinkle over a little mustard and cress.

PREPARE AHEAD
You can poach the pears the day before and serve them cold – they're just as nice. Take them out of the syrup and reduce, then store the pears and syrup in separate plastic containers in the fridge. If the syrup is too thick the next day, add a little warm water, and if it is too thin, you can reduce it by simmering for a minute or two.

Prosciutto and Rocket Rolls

This recipe is simplicity itself. Bresaola, Italian dried cured beef, makes a good alternative to the prosciutto.

Time: 20–30 minutes
Serves 8–12
half a 250g tub of ricotta
2 tbsp pesto (red or green)
12 slices of prosciutto
50g bag rocket leaves

1 Mix the ricotta with the pesto and season with salt and pepper. Cut each slice of prosciutto in half widthways, then spread the ricotta mix over them.
2 Lay a few rocket leaves lengthways on each slice so they poke out at each end. Roll each one up and place on a serving plate. Sprinkle with ground pepper.

PREPARE AHEAD
Assemble the rolls on the plate, cover with cling film and keep in the fridge for up to 2 hours until ready to serve.

Party Punch

It's good to have a choice of boozy and alcohol-free punches. Just make sure that they're clearly marked!

Peach Sangria (right in picture)
Put 2 bottles dry white Zinfandel, 4 tbsp Cointreau, 250ml/9fl oz peach schnapps, 4 tbsp golden caster sugar, 2 cinnamon sticks, 2 sliced limes and 2 sliced oranges into a large bowl, stir and chill. To serve, add 500ml/18fl oz soda water, some ice and pour into jugs.

Virgin Sea Breeze (left in picture)
Crush 140g/5oz cranberries with 50g/2oz golden caster sugar and put in the bottom of 8 glasses. Mix together 1 litre/1¾ pints cranberry juice and 1 litre/1¾ pints pink grapefruit juice and pour over. Add ice to serve.

CHAPTER 3

Christmas Day Lunch

No meal comes close to matching Christmas lunch. It's the big occasion that is replicated in different guises all around the country. Whether you are having a big family get-together or an intimate meal, you'll want to make it memorable, delicious, and stress-free.

The menu I've devised with the *BBC Good Food* team and celebrity chefs delivers on all those fronts. It brings together the traditional elements, adds a few twists, includes a timeplan and offers you alternatives for those recipes that may not be to your taste. With our tried-and-tested recipes and timeplan, you'll glide effortlessly through Christmas lunch.

Cooking is always easier with a little preplanning. The TV chefs know all about prep work and have cookery assistants to give them a hand with ingredients. So, like a true pro enlist a few helpers for vegetable-peeling and sauce-stirring duties.

A few weeks before the Big Day, finalise your guest list and menu. Once you've decided on the dishes, jot down a comprehensive shopping list and order your turkey, wine and groceries. Also, check out our list of specialist suppliers, page 140.

By Christmas Eve, you should only have the fresh produce to buy. But even that can now be delivered by the supermarkets or an organic vegetable box delivery scheme to your home.

And while you're rolling those stuffing balls, don't forget, Christmas is meant to be fun. Don't feel you have to make absolutely everything. You could use our menu as a guideline, and make some dishes and buy other key elements.

I enjoyed putting this menu together and hope you'll get as much enjoyment from making or customising it to suit your time and tastes. Happy Christmas!

Your Christmas Lunch – timed to perfection

These timings are based on cooking a 4.5–5.6kg/10–12lb turkey. Recalculate your turkey cooking times, if roasting a smaller or larger bird.

Two weeks before

Make the Brandy Butter (page 94), cover and store in the fridge.

The week before

Make the Cranberry Sauce (page 79), cover and store in the fridge.

Two days ahead

Soak the fruits for the Microwave Christmas Pudding (page 94).

The day before

■ Make the Microwave Christmas Pudding, if reheating on the day.
■ Prepare the turkey, weigh and calculate the cooking time, plus remember to add the weight of the stuffing, if not cooking that separately in balls.
■ Make Gordon Ramsay's Cream of Cauliflower Soup (page 72).
■ Prepare the carrots (page 83), seal in a polythene bag in the fridge.
■ Prepare the breadcrumbs for the bread sauce (page 78), then make and chill the sauce overnight.
■ Make the Christmas Red Cabbage (page 81), cover and store in a cool place.

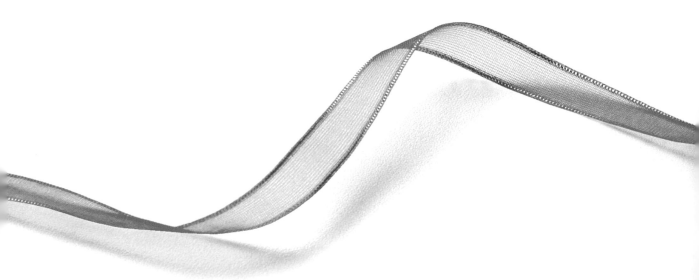

On the day

For a 2pm lunch:

9.15am Make the Chestnut Stuffing (page 76) and prepare the sprouts (page 82).

9.45am Preheat the oven to 190°C/Gas 5/fan oven 170°C. While it is preheating, prepare the turkey for the oven. If stuffing the neck end, recalculate the cooking time.

9.55am Put the turkey in the oven and baste with juices every 30 minutes.

11am Lay the table. Take your prepared dishes out of the fridge and put your white wines and Champagne in to chill.

11.15am Prepare the potatoes for roasting (page 80).

12.45pm Put the roast potatoes in the oven.

1pm Line up your vegetables for reheating on the hob and in the oven. Put your stuffing in to cook, if you are cooking it separately as balls. Take the cranberry sauce out of the fridge.

1.25pm Take the turkey out of the oven and leave to rest for 30 minutes, covered in foil and a clean tea towel.

1.40pm Cook the carrots and Brussels sprouts; keep warm. Gently reheat the cabbage.

1.50pm Start making the Port and Lingonberry Gravy (page 77).

1.55pm Gently reheat the cauliflower soup. Carve your turkey and cover.

2pm Serve the soup, followed by the turkey and all the vegetables.

3pm Reheat the Christmas Pudding in the microwave.

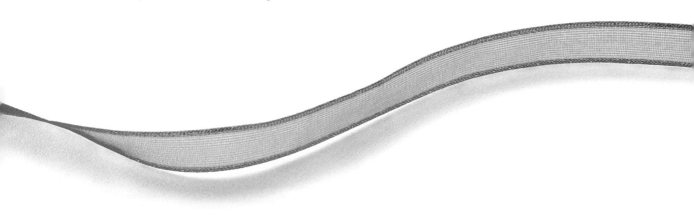

Talking Turkey

Everything you need to know about buying and cooking your Christmas turkey.

TURKEY SIZES AND THAWING TIMES

2.25kg/5lb serves 4–6 (thawing time 20 hours)

3.6kg/8lb serves 6–8 (thawing time 24+ hours)

4.5–5.6kg/10–12lb serves 8–10 (thawing time 25+ hours)

6.75kg/15lb serves 10–12 (thawing time 30+ hours)

9kg/20lb serves 12–15 (thawing time 45+ hours)

FRESH OR FROZEN?

A fresh turkey should be collected no more than 2 days before cooking. Once home, remove the packaging and set aside any giblets in a covered bowl. Wipe the turkey inside and out with kitchen paper, put it on a large plate and cover with foil. Keep it at the bottom of the fridge, and bring to room temperature an hour before cooking.

A frozen turkey will need careful thawing. Aim to have it thawed and in the fridge by Christmas Eve. There are two ways to thaw: either put it in a cool place (below 15°C/60°F) or, to speed things up, immerse in regularly changed water below 15°C/60°F (as recommended by the British Turkey Information Service).

DEFROSTING A FROZEN BIRD

Thaw your turkey in its packaging on a tray in a cool place such as the garage or larder. When it's completely thawed (check for ice crystals in the cavity), remove the packaging, giblets and neck. Wipe with kitchen paper and store, loosely covered with cling film or greaseproof paper, in the fridge at a temperature of no more than 5°C.

ROASTING TIMES

Whether you use your own recipe or one of ours, the method of calculating the roasting time will be the same: allow 18 minutes per 450g/1lb (stuffed weight). Roast at 190°C/Gas 5/fan oven 170°C, covered with foil until the last 30 minutes.

Weight	Cooking time
2.25kg/5lb	1½ hours
3.6kg/8lb	2½ hours
4.5–5.6kg/10–12lb	3–3½ hours
6.75kg/15lb	4½ hours
9kg/20lb	6 hours

Calculate the amount of time your turkey will take:

Turkey went in at _____

Turkey should be cooked at _____

Allow 30–45 minutes' resting time, covered tightly in foil, which means serving time will be _____ to _____

YOUR TURKEY QUERIES ANSWERED

Why shouldn't you stuff the cavity?

It's safer to stuff the neck end only, never the body cavity, as the temperature in the centre of the bird may not rise high enough to destroy any food poisoning bacteria. The safest way to cook stuffing is in a separate dish.

Should I cover the turkey with foil?

It's a good idea to cover the turkey with foil until 30 minutes before the turkey is cooked. This will protect the delicate breast meat and keep it moist, while the last 30 minutes uncovered lets the skin brown and crisp up. The important thing is not to cover it tightly or it will steam – just lay a sheet of foil very loosely over the top before it goes in the oven.

How do I know it's cooked?

If you have a meat thermometer, then this is when it will come into its own. Towards the end of your calculated cooking time, push the thermometer into the thickest part of the turkey thigh, without touching the bone. It should read 90°C for the turkey to be properly cooked.

Alternatively, you can use the skewer test (see below). Prick the thickest part of a turkey thigh with a skewer and catch the juices with a spoon. If they are clear and golden, the bird is cooked. If there are streaks of blood, it is not. Return the bird to the oven for a further 30 minutes; don't keep opening the oven door as this slows things down.

Not cooked: the meat juices are still pink.

Cooked: the meat juices run clear.

How do you get the tastiest turkey?

If you are not cooking the recipe on page 75, where the bird is basted with butter, then it's a good idea to roast your turkey upside down on its breast so the juices from the back and legs run down to the breast, keeping it moist. To prevent the flesh drying out, baste the bird with butter or oil, cover loosely with foil and baste every 30 minutes. Remove the foil for the last 30–40 minutes of cooking time to crisp the skin.

Won't the turkey go cold if I leave it to rest?

As long as it's wrapped and kept in a warm place it won't go cold during the resting time. To wrap the bird, lay a large sheet of foil on the work surface, then put the turkey on its carving board or platter on top. Bring the foil up and over the turkey to enclose it tightly and fold the edges together to seal. You can leave it as long as 45 minutes like this.

What's the best way to store leftover turkey?

Cold turkey can be wrapped in cling film and stored in the fridge for 3 days. It can also be frozen for up to 2 months.

Six easy steps to carving the turkey

1 TAKE LEGS OFF Steadying the turkey with a large fork, cut the skin between one of the thighs and the body, then bend the thigh outwards. Press down on the leg to expose the hip joint, then cut straight through the joint to remove the whole leg from the body. Repeat with the other leg.

2 CUT LEGS IN HALF With the knuckle end facing upwards, cut through the joint between the drumstick and the thigh. Do the same with the other leg.

3 CARVE LEG MEAT Holding the knuckle end of each drumstick, carve the meat from one side following the line of the bone (you may find this easier with a smaller knife). Repeat all around the bone, then slice the thigh meat.

4 DEAL WITH WINGS Wiggle one of the wing bones around to find out where the joint is attached to the body, then cut through as close to the breast as possible. Repeat on the other side.

5 RELEASE THE BREAST If you wish you can make the breast slices easier to remove as you carve. With your knife held horizontally, make an incision at the base of one side of the breast. Using a sawing action, cut underneath the breast to free it from the main carcass. Repeat on other side.

6 SLICE THE BREAST Starting at the neck end, slice the meat on the diagonal, including some stuffing. Lift off each slice by holding it between the knife and fork rather than letting it fall apart, then place on a plate.

Decorating the Festive Table

Sumptuous red and amethyst bring a Christmassy yet exotic glow to your festive table setting. Mix and match your old and modern china and accessories to recreate this glamorous look. As an extra surprise for guests, place edible gifts at each setting.

What you need:

Crisp white tablecloth

Hurricane lamp

Candles in votives

Christmas baubles

Rose petals

Roses and winter greenery

Glass tumblers

Moroccan tea glasses

Large church candle

Cellophane

Biscuits or chocolate discs

Thin ribbon and berry decorations, for tying the edible gifts

WHAT YOU DO

✳ Dot the votives with candles around the table. This low level lighting creates an intimate atmosphere even if you are a large crowd.

✳ Choose red roses for a warm, welcoming Christmassy feel. Buy your blooms on the 22nd or 23rd December so they open in time. Trim the stems and leave in a bucket of water with an aspirin or flower food. Arrange the roses in small glass tumblers and dot around the table.

✳ Divide more greenery and flowers between Moroccan tea glasses and place around the centre. As they are not too tall, this makes it easy for people to talk across the table. They are also effortlessly pretty and easier to arrange than one large bouquet.

✳ Scatter some rose petals and the baubles around the table.

✳ Polish your glasses and cutlery so they are gleaming and twinkle in the light of the candles.

✳ Place a large church candle in your hurricane lamp and scatter some more petals inside around the base.

✳ Wrap small stacks of chocolate discs and biscuits in an oblong of cellophane and tie the ends cracker-style with ribbons and berry decorations.

Gordon Ramsay's
Cream of Cauliflower Soup with Sautéed Wild Mushrooms

This simple blender soup is one of my personal favourites as it can be served simply or dressed up with luxurious wild mushrooms as here, or you can use chestnut mushrooms instead. You can make it up to a day ahead, just cool, cover and chill.

Time: 1¼–1½ hours

Serves 8 generously

1 large cauliflower (about 1.3kg/3lb), stalks discarded and florets chopped

1 large potato, peeled and chopped into large chunks

1 onion, chopped

25g/1oz butter

4 tbsp olive oil

1.2 litres/2 pints light chicken or vegetable stock

600ml/1 pint full-fat milk

142ml carton double cream

250g/9oz wild mushrooms

1–2 tbsp finely snipped fresh chives

1 Put the cauliflower, potato and onion in a large saucepan with the butter and half of the oil. Gently heat the contents until they start to sizzle, then cover with a lid and sweat over a low heat for about 10 minutes, stirring occasionally. The vegetables should be softened but not coloured.

2 Pour in the stock and bring to the boil, then pour in the milk and return gently to a boil. This way, there will be no scum forming from the milk. Season to taste then simmer, uncovered, for 10–15 minutes until the vegetables are soft. Pour in half the cream.

3 Blend everything in a food processor or blender, in batches. For an extra creamy texture, push the purée through a sieve with the back of a ladle. Stir in the rest of the cream.

4 To serve, pick over the mushrooms. Wild mushrooms can be gritty so wash them quickly in a bowl of cold water then drain well and pat dry. Trim the stalks and chop or slice the mushrooms neatly. Heat the remaining oil in a frying pan and, when very hot, stir fry the mushrooms quickly until nicely browned, seasoning with salt and freshly ground black pepper as you cook them.

5 Reheat the soup until piping hot. Check for seasoning and ladle into warmed bowls. Spoon the mushrooms into the centre and sprinkle lightly with the chives.

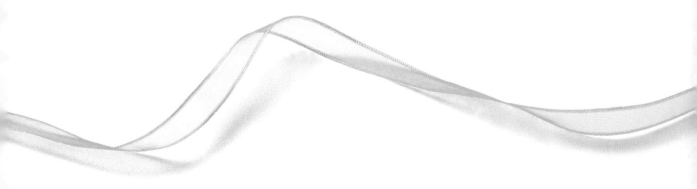

Mary Cadogan's
Classic Salt and Pepper Turkey

I've been cooking the Christmas turkey for over 25 years for my family, and loved every occasion. I've tried lots of recipe variations, but I still think it's hard to beat a classic crunchy coating of freshly crushed black pepper, lemon zest and salt for the turkey. I've added an attractive lattice of bacon rashers and a garnish of bay leaves to set this bird apart from any other Sunday roast chicken, and give it that wow factor.

The gravy also has a special makeover with the addition of port and lingonberry preserve. I recommend you make it as it really holds the meal together. Before you serve, leave the turkey to rest, (see page 69). This makes carving easier and gives you breathing time to finish the accompaniments and enjoy a glass of bubbly.

Time: 45 minutes–1 hour, plus 3–3½ hours in the oven

Serves 8–10 with leftovers

4.5–5.6kg/10–12lb turkey, thawed if frozen, giblets removed

1 tbsp black peppercorns

1 tbsp Maldon sea salt

1 lemon

a few bay leaves, plus extra sprigs to garnish

Chestnut Stuffing (see page 76)

50g/2oz butter, melted

10–12 rashers streaky bacon

STEP 1 Preheat the oven to 190°C/Gas 5/fan oven 170°C. Wash the turkey inside and out and dry well with kitchen paper. Season inside the bird with salt and pepper. Coarsely crush the peppercorns with a pestle and mortar and add the sea salt. Finely grate the lemon rind on top and mix together. Quarter the lemon and put inside the body cavity along with a few bay leaves.

STEP 2 If you are stuffing the turkey, stuff the neck end only, pushing towards the breast. Don't overfill as the stuffing will expand on cooking. Secure the neck end flap with a small metal or wooden skewer. Tie the turkey legs together with kitchen string to give it a good shape. Weigh the turkey and calculate the cooking time at 18 minutes per 450g/1lb.

STEP 3 Set the turkey in a large roasting tin. Brush liberally all over with melted butter. Sprinkle the salt and pepper mix evenly over the breast and legs. Cover the turkey loosely with a large square of foil and roast for the calculated cooking time, basting with the pan juices every 30 minutes.

continued ▷

4 Half an hour before the end of the cooking time, remove the foil and string. Re-tie the legs with a rasher of bacon and arrange the rest in a lattice over the breast. Put any stuffing balls around the turkey. Spoon or siphon off 6 tablespoons of pan juices into a saucepan for the gravy, then return the turkey to the oven. At the end of the cooking time, transfer the turkey to a serving platter. Cover tightly with foil and leave to rest for 30 minutes. Meanwhile, make the gravy (page 77). Carve the turkey (page 69) and serve.

Raymond Blanc's
Chestnut Stuffing

One Christmas tradition in France is to have goose without stuffing. A shame as I think this recipe is wonderful, good for stuffing the bird or made into these delicious round balls. You'll get the best flavour if you use a quality sausagemeat made from free-range pork.

Time: 20 minutes, plus 35–40 minutes in the oven

Makes 24 stuffing balls, or enough to stuff a 4.5–5.6kg/10–12lb turkey

25g/1oz butter

1 large onion, peeled and finely chopped

10 juniper berries

1kg/2lb 4oz good quality sausagemeat (or good sausages removed from their casings)

200g pack cooked, peeled whole chestnuts (vacuum packed), roughly chopped

2 eggs

1 small bunch fresh sage (4 tbsp chopped)

100g/4oz fresh white breadcrumbs

¼ tsp ground allspice

1 In a medium saucepan, melt the butter over a gentle heat, then add the onion and juniper berries. Cook for 5 minutes, without allowing the onions to colour. Leave to cool.

2 Remove and discard the juniper berries. In a large bowl, mix the onions with the rest of the ingredients. Season with salt, pepper and allspice. (*You can make the stuffing a day ahead to the end of this step and keep it in the fridge until ready to use.*)

3 Shape into about 24 balls – this is easier with wet hands – and bake in a roasting tin with the turkey for 35–40 minutes.

TASTIER STUFFING
To make sure you've got the seasoning just right, fry a small piece of the stuffing before shaping, then taste and adjust as necessary.

Mary Cadogan's
Port and Lingonberry Gravy

This is as easy as making ordinary gravy, but with fantastic festive flavours stirred in.

2 tbsp plain flour

600ml/1 pint turkey or chicken stock

150ml/¼ pint port

4 tbsp lingonberry preserve or cranberry sauce

2 tsp wholegrain mustard

STEP 1 Heat the 6 tablespoons of the turkey pan juices in a saucepan. Whisk in the flour and cook for 3 minutes until golden. Gradually whisk in the turkey or chicken stock and port, cooking until the gravy is no longer lumpy. Stir in the lingonberry preserve (or cranberry sauce) and mustard and simmer for 5 minutes.

STEP 2 Taste the gravy and season if necessary. Skim off the fat from the juices in the roasting tin, then add about 150ml/¼ pint of the pan juices to the gravy. Heat through then transfer to a warmed gravy boat.

WHERE TO BUY LINGONBERRY PRESERVE
Made from lingonberries that grow wild in Sweden, you can buy the preserve from Swedish store Ikea or from Swedish Affär (020 7224 9300 for stockists). As well as turkey, it goes well with toast, sausages and meatballs. If you can't find it, cranberry sauce is a good substitute.

MAKE YOUR OWN TURKEY STOCK

This is so easy and adds great flavour to your gravy. Rinse the giblets and put in a large pan with a small onion, halved, a carrot and celery stick, both roughly chopped, a few black peppercorns and cloves, a couple of bay leaves and a few parsley stalks. Pour over 1.2 litres/2 pints cold water and a good sprinkling of salt. Bring to the boil, then reduce the heat, skim off any foam that rises to the top and simmer, partly covered, for 1 hour. Strain the stock into the bowl, and leave to cool, then cover the bowl with cling film and chill for up to 24 hours. It can also be frozen in plastic containers in batches for up to 1 month.

Tony Tobin's Christmas sauces

Christmas wouldn't be Christmas without cranberry and bread sauce, and this delectable duo really knocks spots off the shop-bought varieties.

French-bread Sauce

I wouldn't normally use double cream in this sauce, but I'm making an exception as it is Christmas after all.

Time: 15–25 minutes

Serves 8

200g/8oz stale French stick
700ml/1¼ pints full-fat milk
1 small onion, peeled and studded with 6 cloves
1 bay leaf
generous knob of butter
pinch of ground allspice
3 tbsp double cream, plus extra to serve

STEP 1 Shave the light brown crust from the outside of the French stick with a bread knife and discard it. Cut the bready centre into 5cm/2in cubes.

STEP 2 In a saucepan, bring the milk, onion, bay leaf, butter, allspice and 3 tablespoons cream to the boil. Reduce the heat, then add the bread. Gently simmer, uncovered, for 5 minutes. Add a little seasoning, then cool. Remove the onion and bay leaf. The sauce can be refrigerated in a covered container overnight.

TO SERVE

Warm through gently in a pan, adding extra double cream to give a light, creamy consistency. Grind over some black pepper and serve.

Cranberry Sauce with Port and Star Anise

The star anise has a similar flavour to aniseed and it makes this recipe really Christmassy.
You'll find star anise in jars in the spice section at the supermarket.

Time: 20–30 minutes

Serves 10

*Freeze for up to 2 months

250g/9oz fresh or frozen
cranberries

grated zest of 1 orange and
the juice of 2

2 tbsp redcurrant jelly

150ml/¼ pint port

1 star anise

2 tbsp golden caster sugar,
or more to taste

STEP 1 Tip the cranberries into a pan, grate in the orange zest then squeeze in the juice. Add the redcurrant jelly, port and star anise and slowly bring to the simmer.

STEP 2 Cook gently over a low heat for about 15 minutes, stirring occasionally, until all the cranberries have burst and the sauce thickens and looks glossy. You want to end up with a saucy texture rather than a jammy one – you will find fresh cranberries thicken the sauce more readily whereas the frozen cranberries will take a little longer.

STEP 3 Stir in the sugar and taste. I like the sauce to have enough tartness to make you suck in your cheeks, but add more sugar if you prefer. Cook and then fish out the star anise. The sauce will keep in the fridge in a covered container for 1 week or for 2 months in the freezer.

TO SERVE

Take out of the fridge an hour or so before the meal so that it returns to room temperature, then spoon into a serving dish.

Angela Nilsen's
Golden Spiced Roast Potatoes

I've parboiled the potatoes in a little turmeric first to give them a real golden glow. If you like your potatoes crisp, crunchy and golden, then this is the recipe for you.

Time: 25–35 minutes, plus 1¼ hours in the oven

Serves 10

2.25kg/5lb floury potatoes, preferably Desirée or King Edward, peeled and cut into large chunks

½ tsp turmeric

6 tbsp light olive or sunflower oil

½ tsp paprika

Maldon sea salt

STEP 1 You will probably have the oven on for the turkey. If not, preheat it to 190°C/Gas 5/fan oven 170°C. Put the potato chunks in a large saucepan of boiling salted water, sprinkle in the turmeric and give a good stir. Bring back to the boil, then cover and simmer for 4 minutes. Pour the oil into a roasting tin and heat through for 5 minutes. Drain the potatoes well in a colander and give a gentle shake to rough up the surfaces a bit – but not too much or they'll break up. This rougher surface gives you crisper results.

STEP 2 Carefully tip the potatoes into the hot fat in the roasting tin, tossing with a big metal spoon to coat.

STEP 3 Scatter with a light sprinkling of paprika and roast, without turning, for about 1¼ hours or until golden and crisp. Sprinkle the potatoes with Maldon sea salt flakes and freshly ground black pepper and serve immediately.

WHICH COOKING OIL?
If you want crisp potatoes without too much of a distinctive flavour, sunflower oil is the best choice. To give your roasts a light Mediterranean flavour, use a light olive oil or a mix of half sunflower and half olive oil.

John Torode's
Christmas Red Cabbage

This is one of those dishes that can be simmered away on Christmas Eve, and then popped on the hob at the last minute. Make it the day before, and just reheat gently over a low heat until piping hot.

Time: 20–30 minutes, plus 1½ hours simmering

Serves 10–12

100g/4oz butter

5 rindless smoked bacon rashers, chopped

1.5kg/3lb 5oz red cabbage (1½–2 cabbages)

4 Granny Smith apples, cored, peeled and sliced

100g/4oz raisins

zest of 1 small orange

200g/8oz light muscovado sugar

2 cinnamon sticks

300ml/½ pint red wine

3 tbsp red wine vinegar

1 In a heavy-based pan, melt the butter over a high heat, then add the bacon and fry for 4–5 minutes until just beginning to colour. Remove from the heat.

2 Halve the cabbage, remove and discard the core, then thinly slice. Layer a quarter of the cabbage in the base of the heavy-based pan, cover with a quarter of the apples and a quarter of the raisins, some of the orange zest and some of the sugar. Continue layering until all the ingredients are used, seasoning each layer well. Push the cinnamon sticks into the cabbage.

3 Place the pan over a high heat, pour in the wine and vinegar, bring to the boil and cook for 3–4 minutes. Cover the pan with a tight-fitting lid, reduce the heat to as low as possible and cook for about 1½ hours or until tender. Do not lift the lid or stir, and ensure that the lid is sealed well, but check the liquid level every 20 minutes, and top up with water if needed.

MAKE IT AHEAD
The red cabbage can be made up to a day ahead. Just reheat over a low heat until piping hot.

Gregg Wallace's
Brussels with Chestnuts and Bacon

For me, these are the most Christmassy of Brussels. The addition of bacon and almonds gives them oomph.

Time: 20 minutes, plus 15 minutes cooking.

Serves 10–12

1.3kg/3lb Brussels sprouts, trimmed

large knob of butter

12 rashers smoked streaky bacon, cut in thin matchsticks

200g packet cooked and peeled vacuum-packed chestnuts (see below)

1 Bring a large pan of water to the boil, add the sprouts and cook until just tender, 8–12 minutes, depending on their size. Drain well.

2 Meanwhile, melt the butter in a large frying pan or wok and fry the bacon until crisp. Add the chestnuts and cook for about a minute, just to heat through. When warm, tip in the drained Brussels. Mix and season with salt and freshly ground black pepper.

PRE-PREPARED CHESTNUTS

Chestnuts add that festive touch, and buying them vacuum packed and already peeled cuts out all the hard work of peeling them. We used Merchant Gourmet's Cooked and Peeled Whole Chestnuts available from major supermarkets, delicatessens and online at www.merchant-gourmet.com

Angela Nilsen's
Maple-mustard Glazed Carrots

Maple syrup really gives an extra sweet edge to the carrots. If you use salted butter, the dish needs very little seasoning.

Time: 15–20 minutes

Serves 10

1.3kg/3lb carrots

FOR THE MAPLE GLAZE
50g/2oz butter
1 tbsp maple syrup
1 rounded tbsp wholegrain mustard

STEP 1 Peel and cut the carrots into batons. *(You can do this up to 24 hours ahead and keep them in a polythene bag in the fridge.)* Tip them into a pan, pour in enough boiling water to just cover. Bring back to the boil, then cover and cook for 4–5 minutes until the carrots are just tender.

STEP 2 Meanwhile, put the butter and maple syrup in a small pan. Heat until the butter melts then stir in the mustard. Take off the heat. Drain the carrots and tip them into a warmed serving dish. Pour the warm maple glaze over the carrots. Taste and adjust seasoning to suit.

BUY THE BEST MAPLE SYRUP
When buying maple syrup, choose the proper stuff – that is, the boiled sap of maple trees growing in eastern Canada and just over the border in north-east America. Look for a maple leaf symbol on the bottle. Maple-flavoured syrup is corn syrup mixed with a dash of maple syrup and not the same thing at all.

Christmas lunch variations

We think our classic Christmas-lunch recipes have it all. But it may have elements that aren't quite to your taste, so in this section we're including a few scrumptious extras that you can mix and match effortlessly with our traditional menu. Or you might already have a few of your own family favourites that you don't want to cook Christmas lunch without.

Angela Nilsen's
Turkey with Orange and Rosemary

This is a traditional roasted turkey but with the fragrant addition of rosemary and orange. The orange juice keeps the meat moist and makes it incredibly tasty. Wrapping bacon around stems of rosemary gives them a fragrant flavour.

Time: 15–25 minutes, plus 3 hours in the oven, depending on your turkey size

Serves 10–12

Italian Festive Stuffing (see page 90)

4.5–5.6kg/10–12lb turkey, thawed if frozen, giblets removed

2 oranges

24 thick rosemary sprigs, plus extra for the cavity and garnish

50g/2oz butter at room temperature

coarse sea salt

24 rashers streaky bacon

FOR THE GRAVY

600ml/1 pint chicken stock or water

300ml/½ pint white wine

3 tbsp plain flour

2 tsp Dijon mustard

1 Preheat the oven to 190°C/Gas 5/fan oven 170°C. Wash the turkey inside and out and dry well with kitchen paper.

2 Quarter one of the oranges and put the quarters in the cavity with a couple of rosemary sprigs. If you are stuffing the turkey, put the stuffing in the neck end only, pushing it up towards the breast *(don't pull the neck skin too tightly, as the stuffing expands during cooking)*. Secure the neck end with wooden or metal skewers crossways, then tie the turkey legs together at the top of the drumsticks for a good shape.

3 Weigh the turkey and calculate the cooking time at 18 minutes per 450g/1lb *(see our turkey roasting chart, page 68)*. Grease a large roasting tin with a little of the butter. Put the turkey in the tin. Melt the remaining butter. Halve the other orange and squeeze one half over the turkey, then mix the remaining juice with the melted butter. Brush some of the orange butter over the turkey skin and season with coarse sea salt and pepper. Keep the rest of the orange butter for basting later.

4 Cover the turkey with a loose tent of foil and roast for the calculated time. Brush the turkey every hour with the orange and butter mixture. One hour before the end of cooking time, remove the foil so the turkey can brown.

5 Make the rosemary and bacon spikes *(see tip, right)*.

6 Remove the turkey from the oven and transfer it to a platter, tightly cover with foil and allow to rest for up to 30 minutes before carving, leaving the oven on. Put the bacon and rosemary spikes in the oven 20 minutes before you are ready to serve and cook until the bacon is crisp.

MAKING ROSEMARY AND BACON SPIKES

For each spike, lay a bacon rasher on the work surface with a rosemary sprig on top. Wrap the bacon around the rosemary sprig and lay it on a baking sheet with the join underneath to secure it.

MAKING THE GRAVY

1 When the turkey is resting, pour off all but 6 tablespoons of the turkey juices from the roasting tin into a large jug and leave them to settle. When the fat has risen to the surface, spoon if off and make the darker juices underneath up to 600ml/1 pint with water or stock – then add the white wine *(or use all stock if you prefer)*.

2 Heat the juices in the roasting tin on the hob. Stir in the flour, scraping up all the bits from the bottom of the tin, and cook, stirring to a nutty brown. Slowly pour in the liquid then bring to the boil and keep stirring until thickened. Season with the mustard, salt and freshly ground black pepper. Garnish the turkey with sprigs of fresh rosemary and serve surrounded by the rosemary spikes and roast potatoes.

Phil Vickery's
Piquant-glazed Turkey Crown

A partly or totally boned turkey breast joint is one of the easiest roasts to cook. You'll find them in most supermarkets at Christmas and they're the ideal choice if you are cooking for a small family and don't want any waste. You can add your own touch by making this glaze as it really lifts the taste of the turkey. It's delicious served with roast potatoes, glazed carrots and a spicy cranberry sauce.

Time: 10–20 minutes, plus 1 hour 40 minutes–2 hours in the oven

Serves 6

2kg/4lb 8oz boned and tied turkey crown (see tip)

425ml/¾ pint good quality chicken stock

150ml/¼ pint dry white wine

glazed carrots, to serve

FOR THE GLAZE

1 tbsp wholegrain mustard

2 heaped tbsp creamed hot horseradish

4 heaped tbsp redcurrant jelly

1 Preheat the oven to 180°C/Gas 4/fan oven 160°C. Season the turkey crown well and place in a deep medium-sized roasting tin – you will need about a 4cm/1½in gap around the edge.

2 Bring the stock to the boil, add the white wine and pour it into the tin. Tightly cover the roasting tin with foil and place on the hob. Bring the stock to the boil (you will hear the bubbling inside) and carefully transfer the tin to the oven.

3 While the turkey is in the oven, place the mustard, horseradish and redcurrant jelly in a bowl and whisk to form a loose paste. Cook the turkey for 1 hour, then remove it carefully from the oven. Remove the foil, pour off the stock and reserve. Turn the oven up to 200°C/Gas 6/fan oven 180°C.

4 Remove the strings from the crown and evenly spread the jelly and horseradish mixture over the turkey. Return the turkey crown to the oven and cook for a further 30–40 minutes until it is nicely coloured, but not burnt, basting the turkey with the pan juices every 15 minutes. *(See the turkey roasting chart on page 68.)*

5 Remove the turkey from the oven, cover, and leave to rest on a board for at least 15 minutes. While the turkey is resting, put the roasting tin on the hob and pour in the reserved stock. Bring the stock to the boil and reduce by about half, scraping the turkey juices from the bottom of the tin. Strain the sauce and serve with the sliced turkey crown and glazed carrots.

KEEPING THE TURKEY MOIST

You may find the stock starts to dry out in the last hour of roasting. If so pour in a little water or stock to keep everything moist in the bottom of the tin.

SHOPPING FOR BONED TURKEY JOINTS

A crown of turkey is a joint of turkey with the leg and wing bones removed;
Phil has used a crown that has been completely boned, which you will find in many supermarkets. There are many different boned and part-boned turkey joints available.
Whichever you choose, follow or adapt the cooking instructions on the pack, or
if there are none, use our turkey roasting chart on page 68 to calculate.

Angela Nilsen's
Winter Root Mash with Buttery Crumbs

This creamiest of mash can be made the day before and heated up in the oven on the day; one fewer saucepan on the hob to attend to.

Time: 50 minutes–1 hour, plus 25–40 minutes in the oven
Serves 10

* Freeze for up to 1 month

650g/1lb 7oz parsnips, cut into even-sized chunks

650g/1lb 7oz swede, cut into the same size chunks as the parsnips

142ml tub soured cream

1 rounded tbsp hot horseradish (English Provender is good)

2 tbsp fresh thyme leaves

butter, for greasing

FOR THE BUTTER CRUMB TOPPING

50g/2oz butter

1 small onion, finely chopped

50g/2oz fresh white breadcrumbs (from about 4 slices)

a small handful of fresh thyme leaves, plus extra for scattering

25g/1oz Parmesan, coarsely grated

STEP 1 In a large pan of boiling salted water, cook the parsnips and swede, covered, for about 20 minutes until tender. Drain well, then mash them together using a masher or in a food processor until reasonably smooth but still with a bit of texture. Stir in the soured cream, horseradish and thyme and season with salt and pepper. Spoon into a buttered shallow ovenproof dish and put to one side. (*It can be made up to this point a day ahead.*)

STEP 2 Make the topping. Melt the butter in a frying pan and cook the onion for 5–6 minutes, until gorgeously golden. Mix in the breadcrumbs and stir to brown and crisp a little. Season with salt and pepper and add the thyme. Take the pan off the heat. Spoon the mixture casually over the top of the mash. Scatter over the Parmesan. Bake with the turkey (190°C/Gas 5/fan oven 170°C) for 35–40 minutes if cooking from cold, 25–30 minutes if not, until golden and crisp on top. Serve scattered with a few more thyme sprigs.

TO MAKE AHEAD
After sprinkling over the Parmesan in step 2, cover and keep in the fridge for up to a day, or freeze for up to 1 month.

Antonio Carluccio's
Italian Festive Stuffing

The organisation and preparation of the food is the best part of Christmas for me. I use this recipe to stuff a breast of lamb, but it is equally good with turkey or goose. For authentic Italian breadcrumbs, break a ciabatta into chunks and whizz in a food processor.

Time: 20–30 minutes, plus 25–30 minutes in the oven

Serves 6–8

140g/5oz soft fresh breadcrumbs

3 tbsp raisins

2 garlic cloves, finely chopped

3 tbsp pine nuts

100g/4oz Parmesan, finely grated

3 tbsp finely chopped fresh parsley

3 eggs, beaten

50g/2oz butter, melted

1 Preheat the oven to 190°C/Gas 5/fan oven 170°C. Line a 450g/1lb loaf tin with baking parchment.

2 In a large bowl, mix all the ingredients with some salt and freshly ground black pepper. *(To make a day ahead, mix all the dry ingredients and keep in the fridge, then mix in the eggs and butter before baking.)* Lightly spoon the stuffing into the loaf tin and bake for 25–30 minutes, until the stuffing is crispy and golden. Turn the stuffing out on to a chopping board and serve in slices.

LIGHTER STUFFING
To keep the stuffing really light, use a light hand as you put it into the tin. If you pack it in firmly, the stuffing will be very dense when baked.

Spice-roasted Butternut Squash

If you want something deliciously different to serve with your turkey, try my nutty butternut squash dish. Roasting brings out the natural sweetness of this vegetable and the spices warm things up nicely.

Time: 10–20 minutes, plus 35 minutes in the oven

Serves 8–10

2 large butternut squash, about 850g/1lb 14oz each

4 tbsp olive oil

1 tsp cumin seeds

1 tsp crushed chilli flakes

1 tsp ground coriander

½ tsp sea salt

cayenne for dusting, optional

1 Preheat the oven to 200°C/Gas 6/fan oven 180°C. Peel the butternut squash, then halve it lengthways and scoop out and discard the seeds. Cube the flesh. Put the olive oil in a large roasting tin and place in the oven for 3–4 minutes to heat through.

2 Lightly crush the cumin, chilli flakes, coriander and salt together with a pestle and mortar. Throw the spices into the hot oil, then add the butternut squash, tossing to coat in the hot spiced oil.

3 Roast for 30–35 minutes, turning from time to time until tender and golden brown. Dust with cayenne if liked.

PREPARING SQUASH
The outer rind of the squash is as tough as can be. The easiest way to remove it is to use a vegetable peeler and not a sharp knife; not only is it more efficient it's much safer too!

Nick Nairn's
Creamy Bread Sauce

This cream-free bread sauce is lighter than most but just as rich.

Time: 25–35 minutes, plus 12 hours drying bread

Serves 8

175g/6oz stale bread, without crusts

1 small onion, studded with 5 cloves

1 bay leaf

2 sprigs thyme

1 large garlic clove, crushed

85g/3oz unsalted butter

600ml/1 pint milk

1 Whizz the bread in a food processor until it becomes fine breadcrumbs *(it's easier to do this in small batches)*. Spread the breadcrumbs on a tray. Leave in a warm place for 12 hours.

2 Put the onion, bay leaf, thyme, garlic, butter and milk in a saucepan. Bring to the boil and simmer for 5 minutes, then allow to stand for 20 minutes to infuse.

3 Strain the infused milk into a clean saucepan. Add the breadcrumbs and whisk over a medium heat for 2–3 minutes until thickened. Season well to taste.

Mary Cadogan's and Angela Nilsen's
Alternative vegetables

A trio of vegetable dishes that are quick to prepare and easy to cook.

All recipes serve 10–12

Brussels Sprouts with Ginger and Orange

The sprouts can be prepared a day in advance and stored in a plastic food bag at the bottom of the fridge. Take 1 large orange and finely grate to give you 1 teaspoon of rind; squeeze for the juice. Heat 50g/1¾oz butter in a large frying pan. Cut a 7.5cm/3in piece of fresh root ginger into thin strips, then add to the pan. Stir in 1.3kg/3lb Brussels sprouts, trimmed and halved, and cook for 5 minutes, stirring. Add the orange rind and juice, 1½ tablespoons soy sauce and salt and pepper to taste. Cover and cook for 3–5 minutes until the Brussels sprouts are just tender.

Baked Butternut Squash with Cream and Garlic

You can prepare this dish on Christmas Eve so it's ready for baking. Simply cover and chill in the fridge overnight. Preheat the oven to 190°C/Gas 5/fan oven 170°C and butter a baking dish. Peel 2 medium butternut squash or a 1.5kg/3lb 5oz pumpkin and halve lengthways. Discard the seeds. Cut the flesh into 2cm/1in cubes and cook in a pan of boiling salted water for 4–5 minutes; drain well. Arrange the squash in a prepared dish and pour over 200ml/7fl oz double cream. Sprinkle with 2 finely chopped garlic cloves, 50g/1¾oz fresh breadcrumbs and 2 tablespoons each of chopped fresh parsley and freshly grated Parmesan. Bake for 20–30 minutes until the top is bubbling and golden and the squash is tender.

Potatoes Roasted with Shallots and Bacon Croutons

Lardons, small strips of smoked bacon, are best for this recipe. You can buy them in packs in larger supermarkets. If you can't find them, use smoked, thick-cut streaky bacon, cut into strips. Cut 1.6kg/3lb 8oz potatoes into even-sized chunks, rinse and pat dry. In a large roasting tin, toss with 500g/1lb 2oz peeled shallots (root end left on), 12 fresh bay leaves, 6 tablespoons olive oil and sea salt and pepper to taste. Spread out in an even layer and cook above the turkey for 40 minutes. Scatter over 225g/8oz lardons, then cook for 30–35 minutes until crisp and golden.

Ann Payne's
Microwave Christmas Pud

This recipe from a *Good Food* reader works a treat as the *Good Food* team found out when they tried it in the test kitchen. Soak the fruit overnight, then cook in the microwave in 10 minutes on the day, or it can be made a month before and reheated.

Time 45–50 minutes, plus overnight soaking

Serves 8–10

FOR OVERNIGHT SOAKING

50g/2oz glacé cherries, chopped

85g/3oz currants

85g/3oz sultanas

100g/4oz raisins

50g/2oz mixed peel

50g/2oz chopped blanched almonds

50g/2oz chopped apple

finely grated zest and juice of ½ lemon

4 tbsp brandy

PUDDING MIX

85g/3oz plain flour

¼ tsp salt

85g/3oz shredded suet

½ tsp ground mixed spice

¼ tsp ground cinnamon

40g/1½oz fresh white breadcrumbs

50g/2oz golden caster sugar

50g/2oz dark muscovado sugar

2 eggs, lightly beaten

3 tbsp milk

1 tbsp black treacle

brandy butter, to serve

1 Mix the dried fruit, almonds, apple, lemon zest and juice and brandy together in a dish, then cover with a tea towel and soak overnight.

2 Mix the flour, salt, suet, spices, breadcrumbs and sugars. Make a well in the centre and tip in the fruit and soaking liquid, eggs, milk and treacle. Mix well.

3 Tip the mixture into a 1.2–1.4 litre/2–2½ pint lightly buttered microwave-proof bowl and smooth the top. Cover with cling film and pierce. Cook on High for 5 minutes, leave to stand for 5 minutes, then cook for 5 minutes. Leave for 5 minutes, turn out and serve immediately with brandy butter or leave to cool.

TO MAKE AHEAD

If made in advance, to reheat on the day, sprinkle the pudding with 2 tablespoons water or brandy. Re-cook as step 3.

QUICK AND EASY BRANDY BUTTER

Beat 100g/4oz softened butter until it is soft and light then beat in 85g/3oz of caster sugar and 50g/2oz light muscovado sugar. Gradually beat in 4 tablespoons brandy. Spoon in a serving dish and fluff up the top. Cover with cling film and store in the fridge for up to 2 weeks.

CHAPTER 4

Not the Christmas Turkey

Roast turkey is the traditional choice for Christmas Day lunch, but there are other luscious meat treats, which are at their best at this time of year, including game, duck and goose.

The chefs in this chapter share their favourite not-the-Christmas-turkey meals. To get the most from these recipes, buy the best quality ingredients you can. Talk to your butcher or organic meat supplier a few weeks before Christmas. You'll find addresses of some of our favourite specialist suppliers around the country on page 140.

For something traditional that's not turkey, we recommend you cook goose and Darina Allen's Roast Goose with Potato Stuffing (page 98) is as succulent as it comes. Just remember geese are deceptive in their size to meat ratio. They might have large carcases, but geese are much leaner than turkey and have a lot less meat. This option is best for six people unless you have two spacious ovens to cook two birds. The reward however is rich-tasting meat and oodles of goose fat, which makes the most amazing roast potatoes. Cool the fat, cover and store in the fridge and you can enjoy the best-tasting roast potatoes for months to come.

Pork casserole may not seem your usual Christmas lunch fare, but no one is going to complain when you serve Brian Glover's Pork with Pears, Prunes and Verjuice. It is meltingly tender and a real treat.

Other alternatives include Rick Stein's Salmon en Croûte (page 100), and Ross Burden's Bourbon and Maple-glazed Ham (page 106).

We've also got the ideal solution for those of you who don't want to cook at all on Christmas Day. It's Alastair Hendy's Cranberry Duck Tagine (page 102). Make it the day before and reheat on the day. Now comes the hard bit, which of these delectable recipes to choose?

Roast Goose with Potato Stuffing

This recipe is one of my favourite winter meals and a wonderful choice for Christmas Day. The great thing about geese is that you always get free-range as these birds don't thrive if confined for too long. Remember that geese don't provide anywhere near as much meat as turkey however big they are, but what you get is richer and tastier.

Time: 1 hour, plus 3½–4 hours simmering and roasting

Serves 6 (modestly)

4.5kg/10lb oven-ready goose, neck, giblets and wishbone removed and saved for the stock (ask your butcher for these)

bay leaves, to garnish

Bramley apple sauce, to serve

FOR THE STOCK

1 onion, sliced

1 carrot, sliced

1 bouquet garni (a sprig of thyme; 3–4 parsley stalks; 1 celery stick, sliced; and 6–7 peppercorns – all in a muslin bag)

FOR THE STUFFING

25g/1oz butter

450g/1lb onions, chopped

450g/1lb cooking apples such as Bramleys, peeled and chopped

2 tsp fresh thyme or lemon thyme leaves

2–3 tbsp fresh orange juice

900g/2lb floury potatoes, such as King Edward or Estima, halved if large

3 tsp finely grated orange zest

1 Make the stock. Put the neck, giblets and wishbone from the goose into a large saucepan with the vegetables and bouquet garni. Cover with cold water and bring to the boil then simmer, half covered, for 1½–2 hours. Strain the stock when it is ready. *(You can make and strain the stock up to 24 hours ahead, and keep it in a covered container in the fridge.)*

2 Make the stuffing. Melt the butter in a heavy saucepan, add the onions, cover and sweat on a gentle heat for about 5 minutes. Tip in the apples, thyme and orange juice and cook, covered, until the apples are soft and fluffy – about 10 minutes.

3 Boil the potatoes in their skins for about 20 minutes until tender. Drain and peel when cool enough to handle, then mash and add to the fruit and onion mixture with the zest and seasoning. Allow to get quite cold before stuffing the goose.

4 Preheat the oven to 180°C/Gas 4/fan oven 160°C. Season the cavity of the goose with salt and freshly ground pepper and rub a little salt into the skin. Stuff the cavity loosely and roast for about 2 hours. To test if it's done, prick a thigh at the thickest part: the juices that run out should be clear. If they are still pink, the goose needs a little longer.

5 Put the goose on a serving platter and put it in a very low oven while you make the gravy. Spoon the fat from the roasting tin and save it in a covered container in the fridge – it will keep for months and is great for roast potatoes. Pour about 600ml/1 pint of the strained stock into the tin and bring to the boil on the hob. Using a small whisk, scrape the tin well to dislodge the flavourful meaty deposits. Taste, then strain and serve in a hot gravy boat. Serve the goose garnished with bay leaves with the gravy and apple sauce offered separately.

BRAMLEY APPLE SAUCE

Peel, quarter and core 450g/1lb Bramleys cooking apples. Cut each piece in half and put in a stainless steel saucepan with 1–2 dessertspoons water and 50g/2oz caster or granulated sugar. Cover and cook over a low heat for about 10 minutes. As soon as the apples have broken down, beat into a purée, stir and taste for sweetness. Depending on how tart the apples are, you may need to add more sugar. Serve warm. Apple sauce freezes perfectly, so make more than you need and freeze in small plastic cartons.

Salmon en Croûte with Currants and Ginger

With the ginger, nutmeg and currant centre and warm butter sauce, this dish is steeped in the oldest flavours of our cuisine. It's perfect for a deep midwinter occasion, especially at Christmas. I suggest you have this on Christmas Eve as this recipe perfectly matches the eager anticipation we all feel leading up to the day itself.

Time: 40 minutes, plus 1 hour chilling and 40 minutes in the oven

Serves 6

2 x 550g/1lb 4oz pieces of skinned salmon fillet from a large fish, taken from just behind the head where the fish is at its thickest

100g/4oz unsalted butter, softened

4 pieces of stem ginger in syrup, well drained and finely diced

25g/1oz currants

½ tsp ground mace

2 x 375g packets ready-rolled puff pastry

1 egg, beaten, to glaze

bunches of watercress, to garnish

1 Season the salmon fillets well on both sides with salt. Mix the softened butter with the ginger, currants, mace, ½ teaspoon salt and some black pepper. Spread the inner face (not the skinned side) of one salmon fillet evenly with the butter mixture and then lay the second fillet, fleshy side down, on top.

2 Put 1 sheet of pastry on a lightly floured surface and roll it out thinner to a rectangle about 4cm/1½in bigger than the salmon all the way round – about 18 x 33cm/7 x 13in. Roll out the second sheet into a rectangle 5cm/2in larger than the first one all the way round.

3 Lay the smaller rectangle of pastry on a well-floured baking sheet and place the salmon in the centre. Brush a wide band of beaten egg around the salmon and lay the second piece of pastry on top, taking care not to stretch it. Press the pastry tightly around the outside of the salmon, trying to ensure that you have not trapped in too much air, and then press the edges together well.

4 Trim the edges of the pastry neatly to leave a 2.5cm/1in band all the way round. Brush this once more with egg. Mark the edge with a fork and decorate the top with a fish scale effect by pressing an upturned teaspoon firmly into the pastry, working in rows down the length of the parcel and taking care not to go right through the pastry. Chill for at least an hour.

5 Preheat the oven to 200°C/Gas 6/fan oven 180°C and put in a large baking sheet to heat up. Remove the salmon en croûte from the fridge and brush it all over with beaten egg.

6 Take the hot baking sheet out of the oven and carefully transfer the salmon parcel on to it. Return to the oven and bake for 35–40 minutes.

7 Remove the salmon from the oven and leave it to rest for 5 minutes. Transfer it to a warmed serving plate, garnish with watercress and take it to the table whole. Cut it across into slices to serve.

RICK'S SERVING SUGGESTION
I like to serve this with buttered small potatoes (waxy varieties like La Ratte, Belle de Fontenay, Charlotte or Pink Fir Apple are best) and baby salad leaves tossed with fresh dill, a little lemon olive oil or extra virgin olive oil and some salt.

Alastair Hendy's
Cranberry Duck Tagine

Duck legs become meltingly tender when slowly cooked in a casserole. The cranberries give this dish a distinctive festive flavour. You can make this tagine well in advance as the flavours mingle and mature and the meat improves. All you need to do is reheat it in a moderate oven when you're ready to serve.

Time: 1 hour, plus 2¼ hours in the oven

Serves 4

4 duck legs

1 tsp ground cinnamon

1 tbsp sunflower or olive oil

2 tbsp cranberry jelly

3 large onions, thickly sliced

300g/10oz small parsnips, peeled and halved lengthways

1 tsp each ground ginger, coriander and cumin

1 tsp, plus 1 tbsp caster sugar

4 strips orange zest, peeled off with a vegetable peeler

3 sticks cinnamon or cassia bark

1.2 litres/2 pints hot chicken stock

2 tbsp unsalted whole cashews, lightly toasted

2 handfuls fresh or frozen whole cranberries (about 100g/4oz)

280g/10oz couscous (see tip)

handful fresh mint leaves

1 Preheat the oven to 190°C/Gas 5/fan oven 170°C. Put the duck legs in a shallow roasting tin and rub with salt, pepper, ground cinnamon and the oil. Roast for 25 minutes. Heat the cranberry jelly until thick and syrupy, then brush all over the duck and return to the oven for 20 minutes, until burnished and mahogany brown.

2 Put the onions and parsnips in a heavy-based shallow casserole and sit the duck on top. Sprinkle the spices and 1 teaspoon sugar over the duck and tuck the orange zest and cinnamon sticks around. Pour over 600ml/1 pint of the stock, so the duck sits in a shallow puddle. Cover and bring to a bubble on the hob, place in the oven and leave to murmur away for 1 hour. Add the cashews, cranberries and 1 tablespoon sugar and cook for a further 30 minutes, uncovered, to let the duck skin crisp up.

3 Meanwhile, to prepare the couscous, tip into a heatproof bowl. Pour over the remaining 600ml/ 1 pint of stock. Leave for a minute or two, then fork it through. Leave for 4 minutes, then fluff through with a fork, with extra seasoning.

4 To serve, pile the couscous on to a plate and top with a duck leg, some vegetables, nuts and fruits, then spoon over the rich juices from the pan and scatter with mint.

MAKE-AHEAD COUSCOUS
Couscous can be made in advance and reheated in the microwave with excellent results. Simply cover with cling film, make a couple of holes in the top and heat on full power for 1½ minutes.

Brian Glover's

Pork with Pears, Prunes and Verjuice

This extra-special, one-pot rich casserole simmers gently to succulence, and is well worth the wait. The verjuice adds an interesting flavour that sets it apart from pork dishes that you have the rest of the year.

Time: 50 minutes, plus 2½ hours in the oven and overnight marinating

Serves 4

750–900g/1lb 10oz–2lb belly pork, rind removed and cut into 5cm/2in cubes

2 garlic cloves, chopped

grated zest of ½ lemon

1 tsp crushed coriander seeds

1 tsp chopped fresh thyme (lemon thyme is especially good)

125ml/4fl oz verjuice

8–10 ready-to-eat prunes

2 tbsp plain flour

4 tbsp olive oil

250g/9oz small onions or shallots, whole or halved

600ml/1 pint chicken or vegetable stock

1–2 tsp light muscovado sugar

3–4 pears

500–650g/1lb 2oz–1lb 7oz small potatoes, peeled and cut into chunks

TO SERVE

chopped flesh flatleaf parsley

a little grated lemon zest

1 Mix the pork with the garlic, lemon zest, coriander, thyme, verjuice and prunes in a non-metallic dish. Season well. Cover and marinate in the fridge for up to 12 hours.

2 Preheat the oven to 180°C/Gas 4/fan oven 160°C. Remove the pork and prunes from the marinade and set aside separately. Pat the pork dry, then toss in the flour. Heat 3 tablespoons of the oil in a frying pan and brown the pork on all sides *(you may have to do this in batches)*. Transfer the pork to a large, wide casserole.

3 Wipe out the frying pan, add the remaining oil and brown the onions or shallots on all sides. Remove and set aside. Add the marinade to the pan and bring to the boil. Cook for 2–3 minutes, then stir in the stock and sugar and bring back to the boil. Pour the marinade over the pork, cover and cook in the oven for 1½ hours. *(You can prepare the dish up to this stage a day ahead. Cover and refrigerate overnight. Next day, skim off fat if necessary; reheat until bubbling before carrying on with the recipe. You may need to add a little more stock or water.)*

4 About 20 minutes before the pork is ready, peel the pears and cut them into wedges, then remove the cores. Remove the pork from the oven and adjust the seasoning, adding more sugar if you like. Stir in the onions or shallots, pears and potatoes, cover the casserole and return to the oven for another 40 minutes or until the potatoes are just tender.

5 Uncover the dish and stir in the prunes, then stir in a little more stock if the casserole seems dry. Return to the oven for another 15–20 minutes, until the potatoes are fully cooked. Check the seasoning, then scatter the parsley and lemon zest over the top.

WHERE TO BUY VERJUICE

Verjuice is made from the juice of white grapes. It has a mild tangy, lemony flavour. You can buy it from Sainsbury's Special Selection or from good delis.

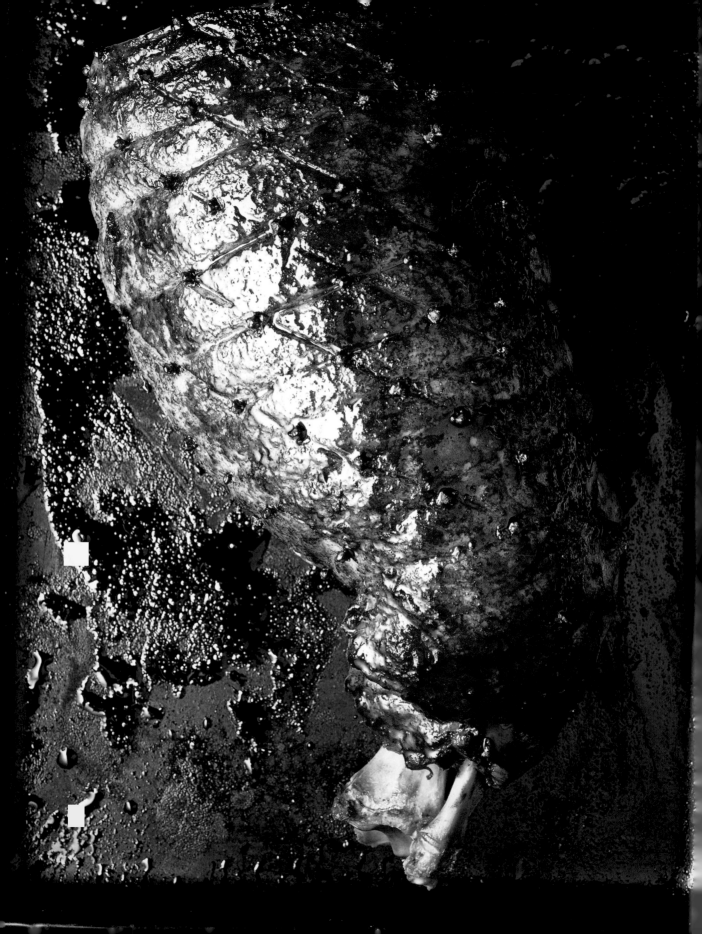

Ross Burden's
Bourbon and Maple-glazed Ham

I've cooked so many Christmas turkeys that I prefer a ham or a goose on the Big Day.
I love serving this ham with candied yams or sweet potatoes. For me, it harks back to the
American south, so once it's in the oven, why not relax with a mint julep in hand?

Time: 40–50 minutes, plus
5 hours simmering and
roasting

Serves 10–12

5kg/11lb smoked or
unsmoked gammon on the
bone (see tip)

1 head of celery, roughly
chopped

1 onion, sliced

1 bundle of fresh thyme

a few peppercorns

a handful of cloves

3 tbsp ground allspice

200ml/7fl oz maple syrup

200ml/7fl oz bourbon or
Irish whiskey

1 Weigh the gammon joint and calculate the simmering time, allowing 20 minutes per 450g/1lb,
plus 20 minutes extra. Place in a very large pan, pour in enough water to cover and bring to the boil.
Tip away the water, cover with more fresh water and add the celery, onion, thyme and peppercorns.
Simmer for about 4 hours *(skimming off scum with a slotted spoon)* or until the bone at the skinny end
comes away freely. Drain and leave until cool enough to handle.

2 Carefully remove the skin, leaving most of the fat intact. With a sharp knife, score the fat in a
diamond pattern, taking care not to cut into the meat. The point is to decorate but also to protect the
ham from the heat when it goes into the oven *(if you cut into the meat it will change the fibre structure
and make it tougher)*.

3 Preheat the oven to 180°C/Gas 4/fan oven 160°C. Pour enough water into a roasting tin to come
2.5cm/1in up the sides. Stud the ham with a clove at the junction of each diamond, then stand it on
a wire rack over the water. Make a paste from the allspice and maple syrup, then work in the bourbon.
Baste the ham with some of the paste and cook in the oven for 1 hour, basting with more paste at
frequent intervals to build up a thick glaze: the water will evaporate, leaving the glaze unscorched.

BUYING A GAMMON JOINT

You can get joints like the one in our picture, which have just the end of the bone left in, at
the butchers. This looks great and is easy to carve. Smoked gammon is slightly saltier than
unsmoked. Soaking removes excess salt, but these days most gammon is mild-cured so it's
rarely over salty. If you buy a smoked joint you may like to soak it, just to be sure. Put it in a
large bowl, cover with plenty of cold water and leave overnight. Drain and discard the
soaking water.

RIGHT SIZE PAN FOR THE JOB

If you haven't got a large enough pan, use a 3.6kg/8lb boned gammon joint,
which will fit snugly into a smaller pan and serve 8–10 people. The simmering time
is calculated the same as for a bone-in joint, so it will be 3 hours, then roast for
30–35 minutes.

Vegetarian Christmas Crackers

Vegetarians are often made to feel sidelined, but this is doubly so at Christmas when all the talk is of turkey.

If you're vegetarian or have a vegetarian guest coming for lunch it's worth making **something special**, but that doesn't mean it has to be complicated. We think you'll find our vegetarian recipes not only look and taste special, but they are effortless to make and won't take up valuable oven and hob space on the day. All four can be partly prepared ahead and reheated or simply finished off. Giving you one less thing to worry about.

Each dish captures the flavours of Christmas and complements the vegetables you are serving with your turkey.

We asked **Paul Gayler**, head chef at London's Lanesborough Hotel, master of vegetarian dishes and author of several cookery books, to share his favourite festive recipe.

He says these Stilton and Corn Polenta Tarts with Roasted Vegetables (page 110) are **real winners** every time he serves them. They are a meal in themselves and straightforward to make, with just the roasted vegetables to cook on the day.

Rosa Baden-Powell, 2001 MasterChef winner and a vegetarian herself, has created individual Butternut Squash and Stilton pies for us. They are wholesome with an earthy flavour.

And if you're feeding a crowd, **Gilly Cubitt**, former Editor of *BBC Vegetarian Good Food*, has created a mouth-wateringly delicious plate pie that's a cut above your standard vegetarian fare. She now runs a hotel in Devon so knows all about the pressures of serving simple but special food for large numbers. While **Simon Rimmer's** Italian Bean and Parmesan Caserole (page 116) is simplicity itself. Whichever recipe you choose, we guarantee your vegetarian guests are in for a very pleasant surprise.

Paul Gayler's
Stilton and Corn Polenta Tarts
with Roasted Vegetables

It's always a challenge to find something special to cook for vegetarians at Christmas, but I think I've hit the jackpot with this recipe. Even meat eaters are keen to get a taste whenever I've cooked it.

Time: 1 hour, plus 45–50 minutes in the oven

Serves 2

100g/4oz prepared shortcrust pastry

225g/8oz mixed vegetables (I use 1 small parsnip, 1 medium carrot, 1 small turnip and 4 button onions)

1 tbsp clear honey

2 tbsp olive oil

25g/1oz unsalted butter, melted

50g/2oz vacuum-packed chestnuts

thyme sprigs, to garnish

FOR THE SAUCE

10g packet dried wild mushrooms, soaked for 15–20 minutes in 150ml/¼ pint hot vegetable stock

15g/½oz unsalted butter

2 tbsp port

1 tbsp dark soy sauce

2 tsp redcurrant jelly

1 tsp cornflour

FOR THE FILLING

200ml/7fl oz full-fat milk

1 very small garlic clove, crushed

50g/2oz canned sweetcorn kernels, drained

25g/1oz quick-cook polenta

15g/½oz unsalted butter

1 tbsp vegetarian Parmesan, grated

40g/1½oz vegetarian Stilton, crumbled

1 First make the sauce. Drain and thinly slice the mushrooms, reserving the stock. Melt the butter, tip in the mushrooms and cook for 2 minutes, then add the port, reserved stock, soy sauce and redcurrant jelly and bring to the boil. Mix the cornflour with enough cold water to make a thin paste. Stir the paste into the sauce, cook for 3 minutes and season to taste, then remove from the heat.

2 Preheat the oven to 190°C/Gas 5/fan oven 170°C. Roll out the pastry until 3mm/⅛in thick and line 2 x 12cm/4½in tartlet tins. Line with greaseproof paper and fill with baking beans, then bake blind for 10–15 minutes. Remove the beans or foil and return to the oven for a further 5 minutes, then remove from the oven and keep warm in the tins.

3 Make the filling. Gently heat the milk with the garlic and sweetcorn for 5 minutes, stirring occasionally and taking care that it doesn't boil over. Blitz to a smooth liquid in a blender, return to the pan and bring to the boil, stirring constantly, then gradually pour in the polenta. Reduce the heat and stir constantly for 2–3 minutes, add the butter and Parmesan and stir until smooth, then add the Stilton and stir in gently. Remove from the heat and keep warm.

4 Peel the parsnip, carrot and turnip. Quarter the parsnip and carrot lengthways, and cut the turnip into wedges. Peel the onions, keeping them whole. Tip all the vegetables into a roasting tin and pour over the honey, oil and melted butter. Toss together and season lightly. Roast for 30–35 minutes until golden and slightly caramelised, adding the whole chestnuts for the last 5 minutes.

5 Remove the tartlets from the tins and spoon in the filling (thin it with a little warm milk if it has thickened). Level with a wet palette knife. (If they aren't hot enough, heat through in the oven for 5–10 minutes.) Heap the vegetables on top. Reheat the sauce and pour over the vegetables. Drizzle the rest around the plates. Garnish with thyme. Serve with Cranberry or apple sauce, braised red cabbage, Brussels sprouts and roast potatoes.

TO PREPARE AHEAD

Make the sauce and bake the tartlet shells the day before. You can make the filling a few hours ahead, but you need to roast the vegetables just before serving. While they're roasting, fill the tartlets and reheat on a baking sheet at 190°C/Gas 5/fan oven 170°C for 15–20 minutes. Reheat the sauce in a pan.

Festive Butternut Squash and Stilton Pie

If you have a lone vegetarian coming for lunch or are the lone vegetarian yourself amidst the turkey eaters, this recipe is ideal. It's easy to make but at the same time special. It can be served with the usual trimmings. Make the filling in advance, top and cook while the turkey is resting, so there are no squabbles over oven space. It's important to use 450ml/16fl oz dishes as this helps support the pastry and stops the pies sinking.

Time: 35–40 minutes, 15–20 minutes in the oven

Serves 2

25g/1oz dried porcini mushrooms

1 butternut squash, about 800g/1lb 12oz

50g/2oz butter

1 tbsp olive oil

200g/8oz chestnut mushrooms, sliced

pinch of dried chilli flakes

2 garlic cloves, crushed

2 tsp chopped fresh thyme or rosemary

1 tbsp brandy

6 tbsp double cream or crème fraîche

50g/2oz Stilton, broken into chunks

50g/2oz walnut pieces

140g/5oz puff pastry, thawed if frozen

1 egg yolk, beaten

THE DAY BEFORE

1 Soak the porcini in 150ml/¼ pint boiling water for 20 minutes.

2 Meanwhile, peel the squash, then cut the flesh into 2cm/¾in chunks. Melt the butter in a large frying pan, add the oil, and fry the squash over a medium heat for 10 minutes, stirring occasionally until it begins to caramelise. Stir in the chestnut mushrooms, chilli flakes, garlic and thyme or rosemary, and fry for 5 minutes. Increase the heat and add the brandy. Set aside.

3 Preheat the oven to 200°C/Gas 6/fan oven 180°C. Remove the dried mushrooms from the water with a slotted spoon, and roughly chop. Add to the pan along with the soaking liquid and double cream and bring to the boil. Remove from the heat, season, and stir in the Stilton and walnuts. Divide the mixture between 2 x 450ml/16fl oz individual pie dishes or small deep ovenproof soup bowls.

4 Cut the pastry in half and roll out each piece on a lightly floured surface until slightly bigger than the tops of the dishes. Lay the pastry over the top of the dishes so that it overhangs slightly, and fold in the edges to neaten. Use trimmings to cut out holly leaves and make berries. Stick them on to the pastry with a little water. *(You can store them in the fridge for up 24 hours at this point.)*

ON THE DAY

Brush the tops with beaten egg yolk. Sprinkle each pie with a large pinch of Maldon salt and a grinding of black pepper. Bake for 15–20 minutes until golden, risen and puffed.

ALTERNATIVE CRUMBLE TOPPING

Try a crunchy nut topping (left). Melt 25g/1oz butter and toss with 25g/1oz breadcrumbs, 50g/2oz walnut pieces and a small handful chopped fresh parsley. Store the topping and the pies separately in the fridge for up to 24 hours. On the day, sprinkle the topping over the pie filling and bake as in the main recipe.

Gilly Cubitt's
Chestnut and Roasted Vegetable Pie

I used to edit *BBC Vegetarian Good Food Magazine*, so know all about cooking for a vegetarian at Christmas. I'd recommend this pie, packed with seasonal flavours as it's satisfyingly wholesome and special, and can mostly be made in advance. The only vegetables you need to serve with it are roast potatoes and red cabbage.

Time: 20–30 minutes, plus 50 minutes in the oven and chilling

Serves 6

1 large red onion, peeled and cut into wedges

1 red pepper, seeded and sliced

1 yellow pepper, seeded and sliced

2 medium sweet potatoes (about 350g/12oz), peeled and cut into chunks

1 large cooking apple, peeled, quartered, cored and sliced

4 tbsp olive oil

2.5cm/1in piece fresh root ginger, peeled and finely chopped

½ tsp ground cinnamon

200g pack cooked and peeled whole chestnuts

285g jar artichokes in oil, drained

2 x 375g packs ready-rolled puff pastry

2 tbsp tomato purée

1 tsp harissa paste

1 egg, beaten

1 The day before, preheat the oven to 200°C/Gas 6/fan oven 180°C. Put the onion, peppers, potatoes and apple slices in a roasting tin. Drizzle over the oil and scatter over the ginger and cinnamon and toss well so everything is well mixed. Roast in the oven for 25–30 minutes until the vegetables are tender and browned. Leave to cool completely, then stir in the chestnuts and artichokes. Chill.

2 Unroll one of the packs of pastry and cut into three equal-sized lengths, to give you three long pieces of pastry. Mix the tomato purée and harissa together and spread it over the three pastry pieces. Roll one of them up and lay it, ends matching up, on the end of the second length and roll that up round the first roll. Repeat with the third piece of pastry to give you a large Catherine wheel shape. Wrap in cling film and chill. Cut the other pack of pastry into three pieces in the same way, this time without the purée and paste. Roll, wrap and chill.

3 On the day, preheat the oven to 200°C/Gas 6/fan oven 180°C. Place a baking sheet on the top shelf of the oven to heat. Stand the flavoured pastry roll on its end on a lightly floured surface and roll out to an approximate 31cm/12½in circle. Roll out the unflavoured roll in the same way to a slightly smaller circle, about 30cm/12in in diameter. Lay the unflavoured smaller circle on a large baking sheet and pile the roasted vegetable filling in the centre. Brush the edges with the egg. Carefully lift the flavoured pastry and place over the top of the filling. Press the edges together to seal the pie and brush with beaten egg.

4 Place the baking sheet with the pie on top of the hot preheated baking sheet and cook for 20–25 minutes until risen and golden brown. Serve hot with the relish and accompaniments.

SERVE WITH TOMATO AND GINGER RELISH

Tip 200g/8oz Greek yogurt into a bowl and mix with 3 tablespoons milk. In a separate bowl, toss together 2 skinned, seeded and roughly chopped tomatoes, a finely grated piece of fresh root ginger and a small handful of chopped fresh coriander. Stir the tomato mixture, apart from a tablespoonful for garnishing, into the yogurt. Chill and when ready to serve, top with the reserved tomato.

Italian Bean and Parmesan Casserole

There's something incredibly sexy about this dish. Casseroles are usually heavy and robust affairs, but this one is light with a simple tomato base, lots of beans and Parmesan-roasted parsnips. All it needs is a glass of pink bubbles, some warm focaccia and the right company. The bonus is you can partly make this 2 days ahead.

Time: 45 minutes, plus
50 minutes in the oven

Serves 6

3 tbsp olive oil

2 celery sticks, finely diced

2 large carrots, finely diced

1 large onion, chopped

2 garlic cloves, sliced

300ml/½ pint red wine

400g can chopped tomatoes

8 sun-dried tomatoes in oil, drained and quartered

284ml tub fresh vegetable stock (it's worth buying fresh or making your own)

1 tbsp fresh oregano or 1 tsp dried

5 sprigs fresh thyme

410g can borlotti beans, drained and rinsed

410g can cannellini beans, drained and rinsed

TO FINISH

8 parsnips

4–6 tbsp olive oil

2 garlic cloves, crushed

100g/4oz Parmesan, finely grated

chopped fresh parsley

MAKE AHEAD

1 Heat the oil in a large flameproof casserole. Tip in the celery, carrots and onion and fry for 8 minutes or so, until starting to colour. Add the garlic and wine and bring to the boil, then simmer for a few minutes until the wine has reduced a little.

2 Stir in the canned and sun-dried tomatoes, along with the stock, oregano and thyme. Bring back to the boil and simmer for 20 minutes, then tip in the beans and cook for a further 10 minutes. Leave to cool. *(The casserole can now be put in the fridge, where it will keep for up to 2 days.)*

TO FINISH

1 Preheat the oven to 220°C/Gas 7/fan oven 200°C. Peel the parsnips, and cut lengthways into fairly slim chips. Heat the oil in a shallow roasting tin, add the garlic, parsnips and salt and pepper and shake the tin around a bit until the parsnips become well coated. Roast them in the oven for 40–45 minutes until just tender, turning once or twice.

2 After the parsnips have been roasting for 30 minutes, reheat the casserole on the hob until hot and bubbling. When the parsnips are just tender, remove them from the oven and coat them with the Parmesan, then return to the oven for 3–4 minutes until the cheese has melted.

3 Spoon the casserole into warmed soup plates and top with the parsnips. Sprinkle with parsley and black pepper just before serving.

Other Fabulous Desserts

If a flaming, boozy pud is not your thing, there are **alternative ways to impress your guests**.

All the puddings in this chapter are spectacular, and each of the recipes can be partly prepared in advance. The Baileys Banana Butterscotch Trifle, for example, can be prepared in a quiet moment in the morning and put aside for 2–3 hours until you are ready to serve.

Some of us would rather not be cooking pud at all on the day, so that's where my **Chocolate and Apricot Pud with Glossy Chocolate Sauce** (page 128) is a winner. It can be frozen for up to 2 months, then defrosted overnight in the fridge and reheated. This twist on the traditional pud is popular with children and I've not heard of any adults turning down a slice, either.

It's always good to offer a lighter option after such a big lunch. And **Shona Crawford Poole's Beaumes-de-Venise Jelly** (page 126) is perfect. Made with a sweet dessert wine, it is indulgent but contains fewer than 160 calories per portion. Alternatively, for calorie counters, offer a selection of exotic fruits and serve with mascarpone sweetened with a little vanilla sugar.

It's a good idea to **choose two puds** from our line-up as we're sure not a morsel will go to waste over the proceeding days. Otherwise, make one and have a bought pudding in reserve. At this time of year the supermarkets pull the stops out in the dessert department.

Make sure you have enough accompaniments too. As well as brandy butter for the traditional pud, have reserves of double cream, crème fraîche and vanilla ice cream.

And last but not least, **don't forget the cheeseboard**. Instead of a prepacked selection, choose several chunks from a good delicatessen. Mix and match them over the holiday, holding one or two back to freshen your board. Serve with chilled grapes and thin oat cakes.

Gordon Ramsay's
Blueberry Clafoutis

This pud tastes even better if you make the batter 24 hours ahead. All you have to do is bake it before serving dusted with icing sugar and a trickle of cream. It's equally good with vanilla ice cream.

Time: 15 minutes, plus overnight resting for the batter, and 18–20 minutes in the oven.

Serves 8

85g/3oz flaked almonds, lightly toasted

25g/1oz plain flour

good pinch of sea salt

140g/5oz golden caster sugar

3 large free-range eggs

4 large free-range yolks

375ml/13fl oz double cream

375g/13oz blueberries (3 punnets)

a little softened butter, for buttering dishes

sifted icing sugar, to dust

1 Grind the almonds to a very fine powder in a small food processor then blend in the flour and salt. Add the sugar, whole eggs, yolks and cream. Whizz until creamy smooth. *(If you're making ahead, tip the batter into a jug at this point and store in the fridge for up to 24 hours.)*

2 When ready to cook, preheat the oven to 200°C/Gas 6/fan oven 180°C. Butter 8 x10cm/4in gratin dishes. Scatter the blueberries in the bottom.

3 Give the batter a good stir, pour into the dishes and bake for about 18–20 minutes or until risen and lightly firm. Dust with icing sugar and serve warm.

ALTERNATIVE SERVING SUGGESTION
If you prefer you can make the clafoutis in 2 x 20cm/8in gratin dishes (or shallow flan dishes). Bake them at 190°C/Gas 5/fan oven 170°C for about 25–30 minutes.

Mary Cadogan's
Almond Cake with Sparkling Clementines

A wickedly simple dessert that's light and moist as there's very little flour in this recipe. The apricots add a juicy and fruity note. For the best results, choose small clementines as the skins tend to be thinner and they usually have more juice. Serve it with Greek yogurt as its slight acidity cuts through the sweetness of the syrup.

Time: 50 minutes, plus 40–50 minutes in the oven and 24 hours marinating

Serves 6, with leftovers

* Freeze for up to 3 months

100g/4oz ready-to-eat dried apricots, finely chopped

175ml/6fl oz clementine juice (you need about 6–8 clementines)

100g/4oz softened butter

100g/4oz golden caster sugar

2 eggs

50g/2oz self-raising flour

175g/6oz ground almonds

½ tsp vanilla extract

2 tbsp slivered almonds

icing sugar, for dusting

FOR THE CLEMENTINES

8 clementines

175g/6oz golden caster sugar

5 tbsp Cointreau or Grand Marnier

Greek yogurt or thick cream, to serve

1 Up to 2 days ahead, preheat the oven to 180°C/Gas 4/fan oven 160°C. Butter and line the base of a 20cm/8in round cake tin. Put the apricots in a pan with the clementine juice. Bring to the boil, then gently simmer for 5 minutes. Leave to cool.

2 Beat the butter, sugar, eggs, and flour in a bowl for 2 minutes until light and fluffy, then fold in the ground almonds, vanilla and apricots along with their juices.

3 Turn the mixture into the prepared tin and smooth the top. Scatter over the slivered almonds. Bake for 40–50 minutes until firm to the touch. Cool in the tin for 5 minutes, then turn out and cool on a wire rack. *(Make up to 2 days ahead and store in an airtight container.)*

4 For the sparkling clementines, squeeze the juice from 2 clementines and set aside. Peel the remaining clementines, removing as much pith as possible and put them in a heatproof bowl. Put the sugar in a saucepan with 6 tablespoons cold water. Gently heat, stirring gently until the sugar has dissolved, then increase the heat, stop stirring and rapidly boil until the syrup turns light caramel, about 2–4 minutes.

5 Remove from the heat and add the clementine juice and Cointreau. Return to the heat and stir until the caramel is smooth, then pour it over the whole clementines. Turn them in the syrup, then cover with a saucer to submerge them and leave in the fridge for up to 24 hours.

ON THE DAY
Dust the cake with icing sugar. Slice the cake and put a wedge on each plate with a clementine. Spoon the syrup over the cake and fruit. Serve with Greek yogurt or thick cream.

FREEZE AHEAD
Wrap the undusted cake in foil and freeze for up to 3 months. You can also freeze the clementines in their syrup for up to a month.

Maxine Clark's
Baileys Banana Butterscotch Trifle

Chocolate, Baileys and cream – a trifle made in heaven. Better still these irresistible trifles can be made in minutes. The easiest way to make the attractive chocolate curls is using a potato peeler or you could just lightly dust the tops of the trifles with cocoa.

Time: 15–25 minutes, plus 30 minutes chilling

Makes 4 individual trifles (easily halved or doubled)

85g/3oz soft toffees (I used Werther's Original chewy toffees)

250ml/9fl oz Baileys

4 slices, about 140g/5oz chocolate or walnut cake, or banana loaf

2 medium bananas, thinly sliced

1–2 tsp finely ground espresso coffee

142ml carton double cream

a little icing sugar

25g/1oz dark chocolate, grated or made into curls

1 Put the toffees into a small saucepan with 4 tablespoons of the Baileys. Stir over a gentle heat until the toffees melt into the liqueur to form a sticky sauce – don't let it boil. Set aside to cool.

2 Crumble a cake slice into the bottom of each of the glasses *(200ml/7fl oz glasses are ideal)* and lightly press the crumbs with your fingers to firm them down. Drizzle each portion with 2 tablespoons of Baileys. Divide the bananas between the glasses, lightly pushing them down to settle them. Spoon the toffee sauce over the banana layers.

3 Add 4 tablespoons Baileys and 1–2 teaspoons of ground espresso coffee to the cream and whip until it forms soft peaks. Taste, and if it's not sweet enough for you, add some sieved icing sugar. Carefully top each trifle with spoonfuls of the flavoured cream and sprinkle with grated chocolate or top with a pile of chocolate curls. Chill for at least 30 minutes before serving. *(The trifles can be made 2–3 hours ahead.)*

STORING CREAM LIQUEURS
If you're using last Christmas's Baileys check the best-before date you'll find on the label as it might be out of date. It usually keeps for up to six months once opened. You can now buy miniature bottles of Baileys, if you are worried the liqueur will go to waste.

Shona Crawford Poole's
Beaumes-de-Venise Jelly

Turn an utterly gorgeous sweet, scented dessert wine into a pretty and light jelly. This has fewer than 160 calories per portion but looks utterly decadent. If serving in glasses, use a tablespoon of powdered gelatine leaves for a soft set, but if you are making it in a mould and turning it out, add 5 teaspoons of powdered gelatine or 5 gelatine leaves. Serve with sweet biscuits, such as *cigarettes russe* or *langues de chat*.

Time: 15 minutes, plus 3–4 hours setting

Serves 6

700ml/1¼ pints Muscat de Beaumes-de-Venise or other sweet dessert wine

gelatine or gelatine leaves (see above)

50g/2oz caster sugar

1 Pour half the wine into a small pan, sprinkle over the powdered gelatine or crumble in the leaves and allow to soak for a few minutes until spongy, then stir in the sugar. Heat the mixture without allowing it to boil, stirring until the gelatine has dissolved completely. Remove from the heat, stir in the rest of the wine; cool.

2 Pour the cool, but still liquid, jelly into a wetted 700ml/1¼ pint mould or individual glasses *(fill the inside of the mould with cold water then tip it out before pouring in the jelly)*. Chill until firm.

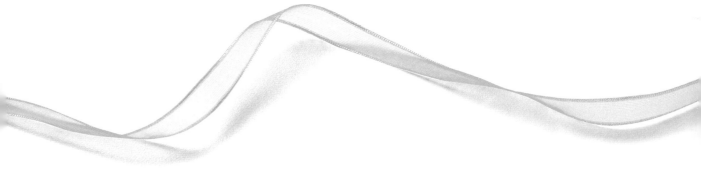

MAKING FRUIT LIQUEUR JELLIES
Alcoholic jellies need extra gelatine for a good set. If adding alcohol to make fruit liqueur jellies, increase the gelatine content by 2 teaspoons or two leaves per 600ml/1 pint. Good fruit and liqueur combinations are crème de cassis with blackcurrants, framboise liqueur with raspberries, and Grand Marnier with oranges.

Mary Cadogan's
Chocolate and Apricot Pud with Glossy Chocolate Sauce

Not everyone is a fan of traditional Christmas pudding and I think this fabulously moist chocolate alternative served with lashings of chocolate sauce is the answer. I've found it's equally popular with children and grown-ups.

Time: 30–40 minutes, plus 2½ hours steaming

Serves 6–8

* Freeze for up to 2 months

200g/8oz ready-to-eat dried apricots

4 tbsp brandy

100g/4oz ground almonds

25g/1oz cocoa powder

100g/4oz self-raising flour

1 tsp baking powder

100g/4oz softened butter

140g/5oz light muscovado sugar

2 large eggs, beaten

4 tbsp milk

100g/4oz dark chocolate, chopped into large chunks

2 tbsp clear honey

cream or vanilla ice cream, to serve

FOR THE SAUCE

100g/4oz dark chocolate

284ml carton double cream

1–2 tbsp brandy (optional)

1 Butter a 1.2 litre/2 pint pudding basin and put a circle of greaseproof paper in the base. Put the apricots in a small pan and add the brandy. Bring slowly to the boil, then simmer, turning the apricots occasionally until all the brandy has soaked in. Leave until cool enough to handle.

2 Tip the ground almonds into a bowl, then sift over the cocoa, flour and baking powder and mix everything together.

3 In another bowl, beat the butter and sugar together for 2–3 minutes until light and fluffy. Gradually beat in the eggs and milk.

4 Chop half the apricots into small pieces. Lightly stir the flour mixture into the cake mix, followed by the apricots and chocolate.

5 Put the remaining whole apricots into the pudding basin and spoon over the honey. Add the pudding mixture and smooth the top. Cover with double thickness buttered greaseproof paper and tie down. Trim off the excess paper, then overwrap in foil, tucking the ends under the edges of the paper.

6 Put the basin into a large pan and pour boiling water into the pan, to come halfway up the sides of the basin. Cover and steam for 2½ hours until it feels firm. *(The pudding can be made to this stage up to 2 days ahead. Reheat by steaming for 1 hour, or microwave on medium for 6–8 minutes.)*

7 Towards the end of the cooking time, make the sauce. Break up the chocolate and put in a small pan with the cream and brandy if using. Warm gently, stirring lightly until smooth and glossy.

8 Cool the pudding in the bowl for 10 minutes, then turn out and serve with the chocolate sauce and cream or good vanilla ice cream.

FREEZE AHEAD
You can freeze the pudding for up to 2 months. Leave out to defrost overnight or microwave on the defrost setting for 8–10 minutes, then microwave on medium for 6–8 minutes, or steam for 1 hour.

CHAPTER 7

Decorating the Cake

Special occasions call for spectacular cakes, and Christmas calls for a centrepiece cake that's a real showstopper. Don't imagine you have to be an expert cake decorator to recreate these looks. Our experts have devised stunning designs that are not difficult to achieve and the step-by-step instructions take you through each stage. The most enjoyable way to decorate is to set aside an afternoon and turn this part of your Christmas preparations into a pleasure not a chore.

First bag your Christmas cake either by making the Festive Fruit and Nut Cake (page 14) or, if you haven't had time to bake your own, buy a ready-made un-iced cake.

It's traditional to cover Christmas cake in a layer of marzipan and then with Royal icing. This helps seal in the flavours and moisture as well as looking good. You can decorate your cake weeks before Christmas, but make sure you've fed it generously with brandy to keep it moist and boozy.

Our three cake designs will appeal across the board. Joanna Farrow's Christmas Crown Cake (page 132) is sophisticated and elegant; Val Barrett's fun sweet-decorated Candy-covered cake (page 136) is one that children will love; and then there's Angela Nilsen's aromatic and eye-catching no-ice Fragrant Spice Cake (page 138) covered in just marzipan and simply decorated with herbs and spices. For an easy, no-ice decoration, recreate the cake opposite. Put slices of clementines and red apples on wire racks on a baking tray in a low oven (150°C/gas 2/fan oven 130°C) for 1–1¼ hours. When cool, thread on to string with halved cinnamon sticks. Make holes in the top of the cake and position the candles. Tie your string of dried fruits into a circle and sit on top of the cake. Finish by tying a ribbon around the cake.

Joanna Farrow's
Christmas Crown Cake

If you like to spend a little time icing and decorating your Christmas cake, this stunning idea, lit with tealights for a festive sparkle, will be both rewarding and look amazing. It's really not difficult, as long as you remember to make the crown sections a couple of days beforehand so they have time to dry out.

Time: 1½–1¾ hours, plus 2 days for the crown decoration to set

20cm/8in Festive Fruit and Nut Cake made without the Florentine topping (see page 14), covered with 1 quantity orange-scented marzipan (see page 17)

1kg/2lb 4oz white ready-to-roll icing

1 tbsp lightly beaten egg white

125g/4½oz icing sugar, plus extra for dusting

3 tealights

small handful silver sugar balls (see tip, over page)

handful silver sugared almonds

STEP 1 First, make the crown decoration. Trace and cut out the template (below). Roll out 140g/5oz of the ready-to-roll icing very thinly on a surface dusted with icing sugar. Using the template, cut out eight shapes *(two will serve as spares in case of breakages)* and transfer to a board covered with baking parchment.

STEP 2 Using a 1cm/½in star cutter, dipped in icing sugar to prevent sticking, cut five or six stars from each shape, pushing them out of the cutter with the handle of a fine paintbrush if they stick, and leave on a baking parchment. Leave in a cool, dry place for 2 days to harden.

STEP 3 Place the cake on a glass cake stand, flat plate or board. Lightly knead the remaining ready-to-roll icing, then roll out on a surface dusted with icing sugar to a 33cm/13in round. Lay it over the cake, easing to fit around the sides with the palms of your hands dusted with icing sugar. Using a small sharp knife, trim off the excess icing around the base. Re-dust the palms of your hands and, using a circular action, 'polish' the surface of the icing to smooth out any creases and bumps.

continued ▷

STEP 4 Beat the egg white with the icing sugar to make a thick paste. Spoon into a polythene bag and press into one corner to making a piping bag. Cut off the merest tip so the icing can be piped in a thin stream. Pipe a thin line of icing down one side and along the base of one crown section. Gently lay this crown section on the work surface and repeat with another section.

STEP 5 Place the three tealights in the centre of the cake so they all touch and the outer edges are all equally spaced from the edges of the cake – this should be about 6cm/2½in. Take the two sections of the crown and arrange on the cake so the bases sit side by side on the cake and one iced side is as close to the tealights as possible or you'll end up with a gap once the six sections have all been arranged. Pipe a line of icing along the base and one side of another section, as before, and secure in place. Repeat with the remaining sections, making sure that an un-piped side section is always secured to a piped one.

STEP 6 Pipe a dot of icing at each point of the crown and secure a silver ball to each. Place plenty of sugared almonds and silver balls around the crown and a few silver balls down the side of the cake, using dots of icing piped from the bag to secure them. Scatter the white stars around the silver decorations and crown; secure others around the side of the cake with icing sugar. Leave to set, then cover very loosely with cling film and store in a cool, dry place, where it will keep for up to 2 weeks. You can also tie a ribbon around the cake. You will need 1.5 metres/1½ yards to allow for a decorative bow.

TO SERVE Light the tealights about an hour or so before you're ready to cut the cake, so you'll have a chance to really enjoy its Christmassy glamour.

ADDING THE GLITTER

If you can, avoid using supermarket silver balls (unless you buy them in transparent packs to see what they look like) as they often resemble dull metal, rather than sparkling silver. Delis, kitchen stores, party shops or cake decorating specialists are the most likely stockists for the best kind.

How to Marzipan your Christmas Cake

This method covers the top and sides of Christmas Crown Cake (page 132).

Time: 30–40 minutes

20cm/8in Festive Fruit and Nut Cake, made without the Florentine topping (see page 14)

1 quantity orange-scented marzipan (page 17)

3 tbsp apricot jam

STEP 1 Place the cake, top-side down on a board. *(The base has a more even surface so will give your cake a smoother finish.)* Cut a piece of marzipan the size of a tangerine and shape into a long thin strip. Place round the base of the cake and smooth in to fill any gaps.

STEP 2 Warm the apricot jam in a small pan and brush generously over the top and sides of the cake. Roll out the remaining marzipan on a surface lightly dusted with icing sugar to a 30cm/12in circle.

STEP 3 Lay it over the cake and ease the marzipan down the sides, smoothing it so that it fits snugly and sticks to the cake. Carefully trim off any excess around the base of the cake using a sharp knife. The cake is now ready to be iced.

SIMPLE SHORTCUT

If you're using bought marzipan, take a 500g/1lb 2oz block of white marzipan and knead it on a clean work surface until smooth and malleable. To flavour it with the orange zest, gradually work it into the marzipan at the same time until it is evenly distributed. It's now ready to use. To marzipan just the top of the cake use a 250g/9oz block.

HOW TO MARZIPAN THE TOP OF YOUR CAKE

STEP 1 Make half the amount of marzipan and roll out to a rough 20cm/8in circle. Trim to shape using the cake tin that you baked the Christmas cake in as a template.

STEP 2 Brush the top of the cake with 2 tablespoons warm apricot jam then lift the marzipan on top and smooth with the flat of your hand to attach it to the cake. The cake is now ready to be iced.

Val Barrett's
Candy-covered Christmas Cake

This is a fun, no-fuss 'throw it on' cake design that children will love. Choose brightly coloured sweet wrappers for maximum impact and make it even more festive by adding candles. All in all, a real showstopper of a centrepiece.

Time: 45 minutes–1 hour

20cm/8in Festive Fruit and Nut Cake, made without the Florentine topping (page 14), the top covered with ½ quantity orange-scented marzipan (see page 17)

about 70cm/28in extra-wide red foil ribbon (or foil wrapping paper)

500g packet royal icing mix

a few rough sugar pieces (A la Perruche brand), or sugar cubes lightly crushed into small pieces

small handful coloured sugar balls

2 handfuls brightly wrapped sweets

5 colourful sugar candy canes

STEP 1 Put the cake on a board or flat serving plate. Wrap the ribbon round the cake and trim as neatly as you can with scissors so it fits the depth exactly. Set aside. Make up the icing according to the packet instructions.

STEP 2 Spread a little of the thick icing around the top outside edge of the cake. Wrap the ribbon around and press on to the sides of the cake using the icing as 'glue' then secure at the join with sticky tape if necessary, to make it extra firm.

STEP 3 Add a little water, teaspoon by teaspoon, to the remaining icing to make it a soft dropping consistency. Spoon most of the icing on to the cake and, using a palette knife, spread it gently to the edges and allow it to run over and down the ribbon in soft snowy drifts. Use the remaining icing to fill in the centre of the cake so that it is evenly covered.

STEP 4 Sprinkle the sugar cubes and coloured balls over the top and around the outside edge of the cake. Decorate the top with sweets and candy canes to give a garland effect, using any remaining icing to secure them. Leave the decorations to set. The cake will keep in a cool, dry place, covered very loosely with cling film, for up to 2 weeks. To serve, scatter any remaining sweets around the base of the cake.

Angela Nilsen's
Fragrant Spice Cake

While it looks sophisticated and elegant, this last-minute, no-ice decoration is easily achieved, even by beginners. The rosemary and spices will fill the air with Christmas aromas. The marzipan makes a nice change from the all-white icing look.

Time: 1 hour

20cm/8in round rich fruit cake

3 tbsp apricot jam, warmed and sieved

800g/1lb 12oz white marzipan

icing sugar, for dusting

5 fresh rosemary sprigs

1 egg white, lightly beaten

caster sugar, for coating

15 fresh bay leaves

5 long cinnamon sticks

cotton thread

2m/2yds thin gold braid

8 star anise

1m/1yd gold ribbon, 3cm/1¼in wide

pin or double-sided sticky tape

1 Using string, measure the top and sides of the cake as one measurement. Spread the jam over the top and sides of the cake. Knead the marzipan until it is pliable and smooth, then break off about 25g/1oz, wrap and set aside. Lightly dust a work surface with icing sugar and roll out the rest of the marzipan to a circle with a diameter the same as the string measurement.

2 Put the cake on a 25–28cm/10–11in plate or board. Drape the marzipan over the cake, then smooth the top and sides, pressing against the cake. Trim the bottom edge with a knife. *(You can do this up to a week before adding the decorations.)*

3 Dip each rosemary sprig in beaten egg white, then coat in sugar. Reserve the excess sugar. Make 5 fragrant bundles: gather together a rosemary sprig, 3 bay leaves and a cinnamon stick, and tie at the end with thread. Join the bundles together with the gold braid, twisting the braid around each bundle and leaving a length of braid between each one.

4 Lay the bundles on the cake so they radiate from the centre, letting the thread loop loosely in between each one; as you lay it down, fix each bundle to the cake with a little reserved marzipan. Scatter a few star anise on top of the cake, and sprinkle some of the reserved sugar over the marzipan. Wrap the ribbon around the cake and secure with a pin or double-sided tape. The herb bundles will keep fresh for 3–4 days.

Christmas by Mail Order

Make your Christmas taste even better by stocking up on the best produce and equipment. We've rounded up the country's top products and equipment, from turkeys to roasting tins and chocolate to cheese.

Turkey/Goose/Duck

KELLY TURKEY FARMS
Kelly Bronze are the top turkeys. They are reared in open fields and fed on GM-free cereals and vegetable protein.
Springate Farm, Bicknacre Rd, Danbury, Essex CM3 4EP
01245 223581
www.kelly-turkeys.com

GOODMAN'S GEESE
Judy Goodman and her family have single handedly put the Christmas roast goose back on the menu.
Walsgrove Farm, Great Witley, Worcester WR6 6JJ
01299 896272
www.goodmansgeese.co.uk

PIPERS FARM
Oven-ready geese and turkeys. The birds mature slowly in cider orchards.
Pipers Farm, Cullompton, Devon EX15 1SD
01392 881380
www.pipersfarm.com

GARTMORN FARM
The ducks here are free to roam about, and taste all the better for it.
Gartmorn Farm, Alloa, Clackmannanshire FK10 3AU, Scotland
01259 750549
www.gartmornfarm.co.uk

Hams

LANE FARM COUNTRY FOODS
Delia orders her collar of bacon and chipolatas from here. Need we say more?
Lane Farm, Brundish, Woodbridge, Suffolk IP13 8BW
01379 384593
email: ian@lanefarm.co.uk

RICHARD WOODALL
Comes with a Royal Warrant seal of approval.
Waberthwaite, Cumbria, LA19 5YJ
01229 717237
www.richardwoodall.co.uk

GRASMERE FARM
Family business selling traditional pork and bacon.
Station Road, Deeping St James, Lincolnshire PE6 8RQ
01778 342344
www.grasmere-farm.co.uk

Sausages/Chipolatas

MUSKS
The late Queen Mum's favourites. The company sells some of the best sausages in the business.
4 Goodwin Business Park, Newmarket, Suffolk CB8 7SQ
01638 662626
www.musks.com

Fish/Seafood

LOCH FYNE
Treat yourself to oysters, mussels and smoked salmon fresh from the loch direct to your home.
Clachan, Cairndow
PA26 8BL Scotland
020 8404 6686
www.lochfyne.com

Christmas Goodies

DUCHY ORIGINALS
Top quality organic produce from the Prince of Wales's estate and favourite suppliers.
Royal Farms, Windsor Farm Shop, Datchet Rd, Old Windsor, Berkshire SL4 2RQ
020 8831 6800
www.duchyoriginals.com

HEAL FARM
Its hampers are a treasure-trove of home-made produce.
01769 574341
www.healfarm.co.uk

SWADDLES GREEN ORGANIC FARM
On-line organic shop of foods that taste a cut above.
0845 456 1768
www.swaddles.co.uk

THE CHRISTMAS DINNER COMPANY
Get your complete Christmas lunch delivered.
0845 607 2512
www.thechristmasdinnercompany.co.uk

FORMAN & FIELD
Sells produce from artisan producers, everything from chutneys to cheese.
020 8221 3939
www.formanandfield.com

CARLUCCIO'S
Stock up on seasonal Italian treats, including panettone and exquisite cioccolata.
Market Place, Oxford Circus, London W1N 7AG, plus branches
020 7580 3050
www.carluccios.com

Cheese

NEAL'S YARD DIARY
One-stop shop for your cheeseboard.
6 Park St, London SE1 9AB and 17 Shorts Gardens, London WC2H 9UP
020 7645 3555 for mail order
www.nealsyarddairy.co.uk

Game

YORKSHIRE GAME
Partridge, pheasant or mallard? It's a difficult choice, or you could simply order a mixed or a festive box.
01748 810212
www.yorkshiregame.co.uk

Chutneys and Relish

RICK STEIN
Pep up your turkey with seasonal treats such as cranberry and orange sauce or pickled chillies and ginger.
01841 532700
www.rickstein.com

Equipment and Foodie Gifts

CUCINA DIRECT
Foodie gifts and top equipment for the smart cook.
0870 420 4300
www.cucinadirect.com

DIVERTIMENTI
Stunning, stylish cookware and foodie gifts.
020 7935 0689
www.divertimenti.co.uk

LAKELAND LIMITED
Clever cookware and foodie gifts.
Lakeland Limited, Alexandra Buildings, Windermere, Cumbria
015394 88100
www.lakelandlimited.com

Chocolates

THE CHOCOLATE SOCIETY
This is a nightmare of temptation for the chocoholic, but a dream come true for everyone else.
6 Elizabeth Street, London, SW1W 9NZ
020 7259 9222
www.thechocolatesociety.co.uk

ROCOCO
It stocks a wonderful range of flavoured melt-in-the-mouth chocolates and truffles. Even the packaging is tasteful.
321 Kings Rd, London SW3 5EP
020 7352 5857
www.rococochocolates.com

Index

Picture credits

The publishers would like to thank the following for their beautiful food photographs:
Marie-Louise Avery: 11–12, 13, 14–16, 17, 20–1, 22, 23, 69, 70–1, 74–6 (top), 77, 78, 79, 80, 83, 88–9, 132–5, 136–7, 139; Iain Bagwell: 26, 28, 31, 32, 52, 53, 73, 120; Martin Brigdale: 98, 101, 105, 110, 128; Jean Cazals: 57; Shona Crawford Poole: 126; Alastair Hendy: 102; David Munns: 43, 44, 47; Craig Robertson: 25, 58, 59, 61, 62, 63; Roger Stowell: 27, 35, 48, 49, 50, 51, 54, 55, 69, 102, 117, 123, 124, 127; Martin Thompson: 36, 39, 106; Simon Wheeler: 76, 81, 82, 85, 86, 90, 91, 92, 95, 112–113; Geoff Wilkinson: 18, 114.
All photographs copyright © BBC Worldwide Limited.